I HEAR THEIR VOICES SINGING

ALSO BY CORTNEY DAVIS

Poetry:

Details of Flesh
Leopold's Maneuvers
Taking Care of Time
The Body Flute (chapbook)
Conversion / Return (chapbook)

Non-Fiction:

I Knew a Woman: The Experience of the Female Body
The Heart's Truth: Essays on the Art of Nursing
When the Nurse Becomes a Patient: a Story in Words and Images

Anthologies (co-editor):

Between the Heartbeats: Poetry and Prose by Nurses
Intensive Care: More Poetry and Prose by Nurses
Learning to Heal: Reflections on Nursing School in Poetry and Prose

I HEAR THEIR VOICES SINGING

Poems New & Selected

Cortney Davis

Cortney Davis (signature)

Antrim House

Simsbury, Connecticut

Library of Congress Control Number: 2020938141

ISBN: 978-1-943826-69-8

First Edition, 2020

Printed & bound in the USA

Book design by Rennie McQuilkin

Front cover photo "Nature & Nurture" by Jon Gordon

Author photograph by Jon Gordon

Antrim House
860-217-0023
www.antrimhousebooks.com
antrimhousebooks@gmail.com
400 Seabury Dr., # 5196, Bloomfield, CT 06002

In memory of my parents, my beginning—
and for my children and grandchildren, my now, my everything

ACKNOWLEDGEMENTS

My gratitude to the editors and publishers of these books in which selected poems in this new collection first appeared:

Details of Flesh (Calyx Books, 1997)
Leopold's Maneuvers (University of Nebraska Press, 2004)
Taking Care of Time (Wheelbarrow Books: Michigan State University Press, 2018)

Thank you also to the editors of the journals in which some of the new poems in this collection were first published, occasionally in earlier versions:

Calyx: a Journal of Art and Literature by Women
Conclave: a Journal of Character
Crosswinds
Ekphrasis
Intima: a Journal of Narrative Medicine
Light: a Journal of Photography & Poetry
ourbreakroom.org
Pulse: Voices from the Heart of Medicine
Rock & Sling: a Journal of Literature, Art and Faith
The Healing Muse
Woven Tale Press

My deep appreciation to these poetry workshop groups: The Hat City Scribblers; The Mad Goat Poets; The Bethel Chapter of the CT Poetry Society; and to these poets and writers whose help, encouragement and friendship has been and is invaluable: Lori Allen, Connie Conway, Catherine D'Andrea, Rebecca Dobson, Mark Fadiman, Charlotte Friedman, Michael Garry, Meg Lindsay, Liz Massey, Jen Sage-Robison, the late Jean Sands, Judson Scruton, Peter Selgin, Jack Sheedy, Irene Sherlock, and Sondra Zeidenstein. Thank you for every red-penciled page, for all those glorious hours. And a special thank you to Gary Metras of Adastra Press for his early support of my work.

My gratitude and respect to those essential workers and healthcare providers—especially to the nurses—who, during the time of the Coronavirus pandemic, raging throughout the world as this book goes to press, daily risk their lives in order to protect and save ours.

TABLE OF CONTENTS

Voices of Letting Go & Holding On:

Voices of Healing / Two:

I HEAR THEIR VOICES SINGING

Ensō

Birth is a beginning, my Buddhist friend says.
Even opening a cereal box at dawn

is a beginning, the way the separate grains meld
into something new, milk drizzled

from a pitcher, blackberries on a silver spoon.
And every breath seems new, he says,

sacred as the morning prayers of the devout.
On my ward today, two patients died . . .

Death is also a beginning, my friend says. It's like
closing out the lights at night to summon sleep—

the possibilities are endless: constellations,
a new moon easing into sight.

Listen, he says, and I hear their voices singing.

Voices of Healing / One

We live in the narrow bed of our flesh.

—Zbignew Herbert

But in the dark pause, trembling, the notes meet,
harmonious.
And the song continues sweet.

—Ranier Maria Rilke

Nursing 101

Silver scissors glistened, the fluted jewel of a nursing pin
nestled against her breast. I was restless,
watching the shirt move over the boy's back

three seats forward. She hushed us, a hiss of cotton against silk,
then she said *pain* and *shot*, and there
in that bright arena, a crescendo of moans like sweet violins.

I learned how cells collide then meld and peel into spheres,
multisided like soccer balls or Rubik's Cubes.
I stabbed oranges until my hands ran with juice, then patients

until my hands rang with grace. I learned the quick save:
airway entered upside down and turned into breath. I learned
to kiss death, my lips seeking those slack mouths while a boy

waited, flicking his bright cigarette, the burning eye that led me,
my shift over, to his embrace. Even there,
I longed for the corridors where patients slept in silence

thick as grief. Where the night nurse moved
in my favorite dance—
pianissimo, pale through hospital halls.

Selling Kisses at the Diner

It was my second year, my wild year.
I was a student on the evening shift, my boyfriend

would pick me up after work, take me
to an all-night diner where mostly old men lingered—

the homeless, the widowers, the boozers trying to get straight.
We would saunter in past midnight,

me in my proud uniform, white stockings and Clinic shoes;
him stopping to slap the backs of the guys he knew.

The old men would sing to me, *I'll give you a dollar for a kiss*,
and I'd take their bills, bend to kiss their cheeks

as if I were Florence Nightingale or little sister to the hookers
who loitered outside the diner door. And yet,

pausing here and there to press my lips to those sad lives,
I recognized the power of my first foray into healing.

Mornings We Rolled Pills into Fluted Cups

Mornings we rolled pills into fluted cups
prim as our caps. We warmed the vial, felt

the resistance of flesh against the needle.
We bathed all those bodies, washed urine from skin

thin as paper, washed young men, all over,
soothed skin that drank up lotion, our hands moving

up the spine, down to buttocks.
We lifted patients, two nurses better than one.

Hands meeting, heads touching, we hoisted
like farmers. Two nurses

make a bed, hands hiding where the sheets tuck.
The sheets are always cool.

Plastic sheets cover the dead—skin
gets mottled in fifteen minutes, cold to touch.

The death stretcher's hard to push,
all covered up, it makes your arms ache.

We held hands with mourners, leaned our bodies
against old men, stood while hands clutched our waists,

pressed our hands on chests, to revive. We laughed
on the way to the morgue, to survive.

Surgical Rotation

He was the first, first death, first cold palm on my heart
hand of frost, pulse of fear, he was only thirty-five, his wife
waiting in the family area, he was in for a nothing surgery
bunion of all things, knobby growth not cancer not tumor
the anesthesiologist gave him the sleepy juice, the patient
went out easy, surgery progressed, skin cut, bone rasp
snips and grinding, nothing, then the gas man gave a little *uh*
and the surgeon looked up, we all looked up, BP tanking
then the storm dam burst, spewed panic like ice
circulating nurse she hit the button and all hell broke, docs
and residents running, me flat against the wall, held breath
bam bam code cart, sparks and the flash of needles, blood stink
names of meds in my ears like static, like shiny wires screeching
then absolute hush, blank eyes, death like a building fell
death dust rose and settled, everything quiet and gritty
everyone with their particular duty, nurses here, there
the senior resident given the task, long walk to the waiting room
speaking the wife's name in his Bombay lilt, her
scream shot all the way back to OR 3 where I stood
struck dumb, enthralled, all of me bright with this
hard desire, *let this be, let this be, let this be my life's work.*

The Nurse's First Autopsy

The senior students said, *don't
look at the face.*

This was a test: weaker girls who
fainted were dismissed. I held my place,
allowed my thoughts to drift

while I observed the race
between two residents who cut
their corpses neatly and with grace.
Organs, scooped out,

sank in stainless bowls. Blood,
once hot, chased
through tortured veins, now stopped.
The doctors drained the heart with ease.
I wondered what

this patient did when living, and yet,
I loved him less
than I was fascinated. Taught well
to separate myself from feeling, I fought

to care *for* but not *about*. Out
came bone from flesh,
the muscles lax, devoid of heat.
I think my eyes burned—then the corpse
was sutured shut.

Psychiatric Rotation

The snow that December fell in drifts
white as our support hose and Clinic shoes
as we slipped our way into the building's steamy rush.
Faces slapped by heat, we climbed to the men's ward
and lined up like children
while nurses in jeans and t-shirts, their keys
a silver jingle, bent over meds or forms, ignoring us.

Finally a man in a white lab coat
led us around the ward reciting names and diagnoses,
what meds worked or didn't, who were the biters,
kickers, screamers, until the charge nurse said,
welcome to the loony bin—that guy is a patient.
Our instructor shared the joke,
passed out our assignments: men with whom
we'd bond, spin words into a "process report"
recording our every question and their response
as we tried out the magic we'd only read about,
dry pages we'd later set to flames.

My guy was young, scary tall, blond forelock,
carried his guitar, nodded at my name,
motioned me into a side room where he played
his songs, wouldn't talk, and I sat, legs crossed,
hands in lap, starched cap, blue uniform stiff
as my cheeks, my heart *poom pooming*
when he stood and locked the door.

The ward outside was blurred by the trick of glass,
a smear of patients, pacing, the faint *chink* of keys,
and me without one, no escape, a bird trapped

in the eaves, a dog chained.
I sat, didn't breathe, didn't flail my wings or howl
for help, didn't move. Sweat damp,

stale air only half drawn in,
muscles locked, *don't flinch, don't scream.*
I checked my watch, and lied,
oh look, all the student nurses have to leave
and I'll be left behind, smiled the words at him,
and he rose, slung down his guitar, unlocked the door.

The next week he was gone, my grade an "F,"
my report blank, only the terror of the silent page.
A nurse with black hair, blue eyes, told me
my boy'd been agitated all afternoon, that night
threw an orderly down the laundry chute, killing him.
Shit happens here, she said, and gave me an easy one,
an old man I danced with that Friday afternoon—
social hour, us student nurses
waltzing with any man not too drugged to move,
old tinny phonograph,
all of us shuffling around the floor to the music's whine.

What the Nurse Likes

I like looking into patients' ears
and seeing what they can never see.

It's like owning them.

I like patients' honesty—
they trust me with simple things:
>They wake at night and count heartbeats.
>They search for lumps.

I am also afraid

~

I like the way women look at me
and feel safe.
Then I lean across them
and they smell my perfume.

I like the way men become shy.
Even angry men bow their heads
when they are naked.

~

I like lifting a woman's hair
to place stethoscope to skin,
the way everyone breathes differently—

the way men make suggestive groans
when I listen to their hearts.

I like eccentric patients—
old women who wear purple knit hats
and black eyeliner. Men
who put make-up over their age spots.

~

I like talking about patients
as if they aren't real, calling them
"the fracture" or "the hysterectomy."

It makes illness seem trivial.

I like saying
> You shouldn't smoke!
> You must have this test!

I like that patients don't always
do what I say.

~

I like the way we stop the blood,
pump the lungs,
turn hearts off and on with electricity.

I don't like when it's over
and I realize

I know nothing.

~

I like being the one to give bad news—
I am not embarrassed by grief.

I like the way patients gather their hearts,
their bones, their arms and legs
that have spun away momentarily.

At the end of the gathering they sigh
and look up.

~

I like how dying patients become beautiful.

Their eyes concentrate light. Their skin
becomes thin and delicate as fog.
Nothing matters anymore
but sheets, pain, a radio, the time of day.

~

I like staying with patients as they die.

First they are living,
then something comes up from within
and moves from them.

They become vacant and yet
their bodies are heavy
and sink into the sheets.

Emptiness is seen first
in the eyes, then in the hands.

~

I like taking care of patients
and I like forgetting them,

going home and sitting on my porch
while they stand away from me
talking among themselves.

I like how they look back
when I turn their way.

The Condition of the World, August 1997

Channel 4 says latex kills slowly—
cameras zoom close to the doctor whose gloves

snap white powder into the air. *First red blotches, then asthma,*
then, in the middle of the night, you're choking.

Next day, my favorite patient delivers by C-section.
Hours later, her belly hard, fever 104,

she's opened again—
it seems one artery kept bleeding, sullied her gut.

Her uterus fell apart and her bladder crumbled
under the knife. *Now she's beautiful on the outside,*

ugly as sin inside. Black tubes drain
her body fluids into glass jars; everything

reminds me of tragedy. In Texas, coyotes howl
at the Green Corn Moon and yesterday on the news,

a Korean boy stepped on a land mine—
the explosion dissected him like flying scissors. In Kansas,

a farmer's wife shakes dimes from a coffee can
and down the road, college girls working part time at US Healthcare

make life and death decisions. Sometimes I beg them all day
to allow one damn visit to the old woman left

balanced on a bedpan. Tonight, TV commercials
resemble acid dreams: starved models walk

into black & white surf, blonde kids
yearn for their fathers. Outside, it starts to rain,

a splashing against glass like blood drops
or the thin fluid wrung from crushed cells.

Once, a surgeon let me place my two gloved hands
against a dying man's heart. The heart, slightly tipped,

lub dubbed like a fetal kitten in a red silk sack.
How clean the body was, split open.

Women's Clinic

She digs callused heels
into the stirrups. Under the sheets, her legs
jut up like ghosts.

I aim the focused glow of light
between the patient's knees—
a scar etches her thighs

like a strand of knotted pearls,
a gift from the man
whose child she carries.

Next patient is a skinny girl
just fourteen,
her mother standing in the corner.

My hand inside finds
the hard rim of the baby
ten weeks along, and the mother,

raving, *this is all I need!*
Big, sudsy bucket of speculums,
I drop in one more.

Now a girl with earrings round as moons,
their nimbus casting
shadows across the small breasts her old man

found inviting once too often.
I grease two gloved fingers, slip over lateral spines,
thrust back to outline her womb.

Outside, other nervous girls are waiting.
They imagine their babies;
they're already inventing their diminutive names.

Alchemy

The sixteen-year-old with dark eyes slouches on the exam table,
    says she wants to keep the pregnancy, says
    she knows her life will change.

Her mother sits straight in her chair and tells the daughter,
    you should terminate. The girl catches a breath.
    Does the mother remember what it was like
    before the first flutter, before the belly grew?

The mother cries, and we think she might strike her daughter.
    The daughter asks, *would you have gotten rid of me?*
    Then she becomes lean, slides off the table, becomes a wolf.
    She turns her thin nose to look at us.

None of us try to guess what will happen. The mother does love
    her daughter; the daughter loves her unborn child.
    At night, howling winds will keep them awake.
    They'll walk through snow too cold for any living thing.

The waiting room is crowded. Little girls with newborn babies,
    flowered headbands wrapped tight around their skulls.

Every Day, the Pregnant Teenagers

assemble at my desk, backpacks
jingling, beepers on their belts like hand grenades,
and inside, their babies
swirl like multicolored pinwheels in a hurricane.

The girls raise too-big smocks, show me
the stretched-tight skin
from under which a foot or hand thumps,
knocks, makes the belly wobble.

A girl strokes her invisible child,
recites all possible names, as if a name
might carry laundry down the street or fix
a Chevrolet. I measure months

with a paper tape, maneuver the cold stethoscope
that lifts a fetal heart-*swoosh* into air.
Then, shirts billowing like parachutes,
the girls fly to Filene's where infant shoes,

on sale, have neon strobes and satin bows—*oh,*
Renee, Shalika, Blanca, Marie,
the places you'll go, the places you'll go!

Nunca Tu Alma

I turn my eyes from the girls' thin bodies
in Sarajevo and from corpses that float down river
like matchsticks, but here in the clinic
I sit with Maya—a twelve-year-old, raped
by her sister's friend—who asks me, *am I still a virgin?*
I examine her crimson vagina. Three
delicate tears lace her perineum, as if Maya
has had a rough delivery.
I culture for GC, chlamydia, draw blood
for pregnancy, HIV.
Am I still a virgin? she asks, her voice disembodied
above her knees, bent and open,
her hips narrow as a boy's beneath the sheet.
I struggle with mechanical vs. emotional, consider
the penis as metaphor. When we're finished,
Maya and I lean close, face to face.
Virginity is a matter of love, I say, *when you give yourself*
out of joy. Rape takes only your body, never your soul.
Maya nods, repeats this in Spanish
to her mother and sister, three dark women
singing like birds. Maya imitates me, her fist
strikes her palm: *Nunca, nunca tu alma.*
Her tests are negative.
Maya's more like thirty than twelve,
the nurse whispers. I crumple the sheet
and dump the bloody swabs,
shove the metal stirrups into the table, out of sight.

Examining the Abused Woman

Her face, when she turns, is like a peach
left in the refrigerator drawer too long,

nose and cheek caved in, as if underneath
the fleshy matrix has been chewed away.

When I ask past medical history, she lists
the broken bones:

Humerus, ulna, sternum, nose. Jaw, twice,
eye socket, she points, *here.*

I palpate her face, dip my fingers
in the little valley of the clavicle, scared

to press too hard. I see her bare.
She breathes, I listen with a stethoscope,

her breath like wind drawn down a New York alleyway.
All the time we talk.

I memorize her puffy feet, her pubic hair,
the scars that rise like topographic maps

across her abdomen. Hand slicked
with lubricant, I probe to touch her ovaries,

hold her uterus between my open palms.
She says she lives in Westchester, a home of sorts.

I finish the exam. She dresses and, not looking up,
thanks me for being kind.   How could I say

It's no use to hate or *I bless you with my fingertips?*
It's me who is afraid.

The Good Nurse

A good nurse kisses her patients
when she says good night.
                    —Elie Wiesel

Our kiss is in gratitude
for rumpled sheets, the hourly
turning of patients. For pillows
placed between legs,

cotton booties pulled over raw heels,
and in thanksgiving
for the patients' needs—
their thirst quelled

by our cold glass;
their pain,
sharp and relentless as a bee
charmed by our fingertips.

The kiss has everything to do
with sons who look at us
and disappear, daughters
who line their eyes with blue

and borrow our too-loud laughter.
We want to bind them
in our arms. Instead, we tend
the patient who longs for us.

He knows we will rush to him,
stroking his earlobe, kissing lightly
his eyelid, his cheek—

not for love,

but for what is constant:
The way skin hurries
to bruise, and the last gaze
freezes the mind.

The Body Flute

O my body! I dare not desert the likes of you
in other men and women, nor the likes
of the parts of you.
                              —Walt Whitman

I go on loving the flesh
after you die.
I close your eyes
bathe your bruised limbs
press down the edges of tape
sealing your dry wounds.

I walk with you to the morgue
and pillow your head
against the metal drawer. To me
this is your final resting place.
Your time with me
is the sum of your life.

~

I have met your husbands and wives
but I know who loved you most,
who owned the sum
of your visible parts.
The doctor and his theory
never owned you.

Nor did "medicine" or "hospital"
ever own you.
Couldn't you, didn't you
refuse tests, refuse to take your medicine?

But I am the nurse
of childhood's sounds in the night,
nurse of the washrag's sting
nurse of needle and sleep
nurse of lotion and hands on skin
nurse of the flashlight beam at 3 a.m.

I know the privacy of vagina and rectum
I slip catheters into openings
I clean you like a mother does.

That which you allow no one,
you allow me.

~

Who sat with you that night?
Your doctor was asleep,

your husband was driving in.
Your wife took a few things

home to wash, poor timing,
but she had been at your side for days.

Your kids? They could be anywhere,
even out with the vending machines

working out just how much
you did or didn't do for them.

~

You waited
until you were alone

with me. You trusted

that I could wait and not be
frightened away.
That I would not expect

anything of you—
not bravery or anger, not even
a good fight.

At death,
you become wholly mine.

~

I inhale, incorporating you
into memory.
Your body

silvery and still on the bed,
your lips fluttering into blue.
I take my hand away from yours.

My other hand lingers, traces
your finger from the knucklebone
to the sheets

into which your body sinks,
my lips over yours,
my cheek near the blue

absence of your breath,
my hands closing
the silver stops of your eyelids.

Voices of Home

I invite you into the house of my past,
and the threshold you cross leads you into your own.

—Nancy Mairs

Something subtle and profound happens when you turn
and look back at the road you have traveled.

—Dulce María Loynaz

The Smoke We Make Pictures Of

Wrapping presents, I look up
and see the clock in the mirror,
how it seems to tick backwards.

In the living room, gifts unwrap,
ribbons recoil on their spools;
my life peels like a time-lapse flower.

I haven't yet met you.
My first marriage falls apart,
my children's legs telescope into their bodies

and they scamper away, curl
like the ends of unused ribbon.
I feel them drawn into me; my water,

splashed at the doctor's shoes, gathers
and the sack seals. For a moment
I think we could start again,

but the hands click back,
the cells of my children shrink
into droplets. Sperm swim, frantic,

and disappear into my husband.
I am free. My hair grows long,
I'm in college throwing water balloons—

they explode, spray rises
and settles like sequins.
Now I'm in my yard in Pittsburgh,

the sprinkler waves a shimmering barrier,
my bare feet print the grass.
Father, just balding,

laughs and lights a cigarette.
Mother, tall and pretty in her housedress,
her dark glasses black as night,

comes out with Zipper. He wags his tail
and smacks his jaws at the mist falling.
I'm so happy I want to stop the hands,

but they inch back and I'm three, sitting
by the mantel, Father snapping a Kodak
as I frown up, waiting for Santa.

I don't know that Mother's just home
from the doctor, her lung cradling
its dark spot, returned from the jar

where it will rest thirty years later.
Father's arms with their spotty freckles
rewind the film, undoing the knot of cancer

drifting in his colon, scattering the pages
of the novel he wants to write,
but never will. Then I spiral into myself,

disappear into Mother's angular hips.
Her uterus bulges under the hot fuchsia skirt
my father loved. It's the weekend he was home

on leave. As they lie pressed together,
he takes back that part of me he will love most:
the way I draw horses with manes flying up

like blackbirds, frightened, rising in unison.
With the final gasp of their union,
I am gone.

Father reaches for a match.
They talk about how I'll be theirs someday,
and they watch the clock on the bureau

tick, each of them exhaling smoke into air,
clouds they make pictures of. *A house
at Christmas. A dog. A little girl.*

Blood Clot

I got sleepy, my right side
became lazy, then wouldn't move.
Inside my lids a plush curtain
turned my friend's face
into a ripe tomato. Mother's
purple violets against the porcelain
kitchen sink became that thick pulse
stopped in my brain. At twelve
I never wanted to be a nurse,
but head down on my arms at the table,

I sensed the potential in disorder.
My friend chattered to keep me awake
while my father phoned the doctor.
When he said *Emergency*, Dad opened
a can of Campbell's Bean and Bacon soup,
stirred it slowly in Mom's enamel pan.
Keep talking, he told my friend,
while I obediently spooned,
with my good left hand, the dusty aftertaste
of soup he'd make me finish first,

when all I wanted were alarms,
women in white bright enough to burn
running with me in their arms.
When at last I was delivered
to their headlong rush, their quick
needle in my vein, their silent
bedside vigil I could count on, I vowed
I would always love their way: Fierce.
Physical. Then they returned me, healed,
to that damn, calm kitchen.

Four Masks

The mask I see in the mirror:

Thin eyebrows. Nose
off center. A woman who has come
to love silence, who sees
life through prisms, hexagonal
planes like the vision
of flying insects, so much color
breaking against reason.

The mask I wore for my mother:

Bright in the way of silk roses,
more than once it threw dinner
crashing to the floor and yet
was afraid to disobey.
At night it stood at the top of the long stairs
just to hear her talking.

The mask I swore my mother wore:

Small clouds like lace
on the brow. Eyepieces
I couldn't see through.
Even her small shoulders
could make me cry. When she died
I saw her face.

The mask I passed on to my children:

Comes late for dinner
and leaves early, clears the dishes quickly.

This mask
is all relatives alive or dead,
drunk, sober, or beautiful. Oh God, *yes*,
at least beautiful.
Everyone at the table finds a window,
stares intently through.

In High School, I Was Obedient

Especially to my mother's wish for me—
gentility, purpose, poise—yet
I felt no remorse the night I escaped,
stuffed pillows in my bed to make a sleeping shape,
my body-double left in case she checked,
and at 1 a.m. rolled the Plymouth down the driveway,
picked up a friend whose name I can't remember,
and in the dark drove to a boys' prep school party
where we drank and danced until my good self, watching
from across the room, made me feel not just alone
but deeply false, a sorrow
matched only by the emptiness I felt when,
at home again, I knew my mother had never looked
to see if I was sleeping, free of nightmares in my bed,
or noticed my dusky eyes that morning in the kitchen.

This brief absence, from myself and from her,
became a story I planned to carry
to my grave. But here it is, a rift so slight
it seems silly to put it into words—
yet aren't there a hundred tiny moments that haunt us
even now, even now?

Entering My Parents' Home

Entering my parents' home
I become weightless.
Mom and Dad don't notice.
Mom—in her summer shorts,
her thin, still-shapely legs
blue-veined as a newborn's head—
opens a drawer,
rearranges a tangle of keys,
adjusts, jingles,
closes the drawer again.

Dad in his chair, kingdom
of phone and pencils, crossword puzzles
and a spiral book of recorded events:
> *July 7. Mother says "My star wars is broken"*
> *in response to "How do you feel?"*
> *July 8. Mother pours a glass of water over her hair.*

Tick Tock, my mother sings,
and the grandfather clock with the broken chime
keeps time. In this house every Christmas
we drank wine; my father
carved the turkey with such care
the slices bowed before his knife.
Over there was the tree.
I loved the shiny wrapping,
learned to wait the long, precise time
until my turn.

Open close, open close.
Mother sings and jingles while father

works his puzzle, searching for words
he knows by heart—proof
that horizontals mesh with verticals;
that sound and shape might be
locked forever into sense.

Washing Mother's Hair

1.

Houses disappeared in snow,
and pine trees tossed down sparrows
frozen to their bones.
We buried them in shoebox graves—
birds' ghosts, like my prayers,
puffed into air.

At night, we'd watch as cars
slid sideways down our icy road.
Deadman's Hill, my mother said,
then she'd comb my hair,

her thin black comb following her hand
until my hair sparked stars
that melted everywhere.

2.

November's winds increase
and sparrows reappear as black-winged geese.

Yesterday,
we washed my mother's hair.

Hold her head above the pan,
I told him, and my father held

her baby-skull. Warm water
from the pitcher; thin, gray hair.

Tonight, the first fog of snow
into which geese and memories disappear,

and my mother, my star,
half-seen, then vanishing.

The Last Heartbeat

The minutes dragged. She worked at it—
sweat pooled in her frown, her lungs
bellowed in and out as if the air were oil.

Her expression never changed.
Beneath the light,
my mother's skin looked violet.

I squeezed her hand,
pressed her fingertips, stroked the branching veins,
but . . . nothing. And so, good nurse,

I held her wrist between my fingertips and counted
one, two, three. Then the last beat came
just as light travels from a star

even when the star has blinked away.
I half-rose from the bed, a nurse
who'd watched her patient's respirations fail—

dumb, slow lungs, they push and pull.
Sometimes, a friend and I
walk in the local cemetery, the graves old

and vandalized. Does a child in utero
sense the blood's first rush? And does
the final pulse release the soul?

Mother's Gloves

I wear latex gloves
to keep patients' germs away—
staph, herpes, HIV—every viral song,
each bacterial worry.

Accustomed to such risky love,
I rummage drawers at home
to unearth warmer gloves:
blue calfskin, the silky buttoned bone

or ivory elbow length I found
in Mother's coat, now my own.
Are we bound
to work, age, sicken, die

alone—not skin to skin?
How can it be? I, who can't remember
Mother's hugs, find my fingers in-
side Mother's gloves.

I Wear Her Red Coat Home

On the day we bury her, I wear Mother's red coat. Her coffin
shines in the sun. I leave white gladiolas wrapped in violet paper
on the coffin's arch, her last face fixed in my mind. A southern
wind turns November's grass to spring, her favorite season,
when, she said, birds sing themselves to sleep.

When I was a child playing in the woods, I learned the trick of
forgetting her completely—cheek turned away, silence in the
face of interrogation, fears so unacknowledged that even I've
forgotten them. No feral child could have needed a mother less.

The coffin is lowered, and I am led away. I carry for her that dry
black void, the one that starts in childhood, rending the gut as if
it were a wet paper bag, eventually blowing open the uterus until
it balloons and scatters eggs like silk, then closes apologetically,
the way dandelions close at the end of day.

I wear her red coat home.

When My Father's Breathing Changed

When my father's breathing changed
from the harsh, regular rhythms I was used to
to the deep chuffing of an engine
struggling uphill in the Pennsylvania mountains
there was no turning back. His body
had already narrowed into a flute of wood,
the sheets damp with three day's death watch,
his heart hammering under thin ribs
like hard steel rams earth in the dry lands.
When pain struck, as if the hands
of the bedside clock were fists beating
each slow second into him, I stroked his forehead,
thought if he didn't die I'd go mad,
if he did, I'd stop breathing too.
Then my father's heart slammed into silence
like a child playing statue.
His skin shrank, the hands turned stone,
only the eyelids were still supple and they flew open.
The hazel orbs of my father's eyes
locked onto mine and all his history
transported itself into me like cargo slid down
into a ship's empty hold.
One breath, two, the lungs drained themselves,
the eyes let go their visions. The spirit
rose, invisible but palpable, and I called his wife
into the nursery of my orphanage.

Any Life

Take the Beatles, the shaggy four, rides home from college, the blond boy driving.

Take the Texas dust, the rattler crushed beneath the tires, the hollow body of the scorpion.

Take the girl child born when cactus bloomed, the record player blasting, window open to the summer air. The years in nursing school.

Take the affairs, the wild ride, *Hey Jude* on the radio.

Take men on the moon and good-night moon, the baby boy and a man home from Vietnam.

Take drugs, Yoko Ono crying in New York, children sitting on a gray VW's running board.

Take *Strawberry Fields Forever* playing at the pizza joint, the new harsh lines around your eyes. The friend who died.

Take the nursing home, Dad's cardboard boxes packed and moved, the vinyl disks sold for fifty cents.

Take November rattling the bones, children grown and mother gone.

Take Ringo's voice singing *good night, sleep tight, close your eyes and I'll close mine.*

Take a slow walk alone the evening of another day. Take your time.

In Mother's House

We have one home, the first, and leaving that one,
the having and leaving go on together.

—John Updike

I find her lotion—
a small glass jar in a kitchen drawer.
The lid is gold and rusted shut.

Mother's T-shirt
is crumpled in the cupboard
behind cans of beans and peas,
a yellow stain on the sleeve.

Upstairs, in a speckled glass,
her toothbrush, white and sitting bristle up.
It was inside that warm cavern,
her last black O.

Here is her necklace,
real pearls she hid in a shoebox
it took forever to find.

And her scrapbook,
clippings of boys with pompadours
who once signed their names
on her dance card.

Over there, in a photo,
she wears a veiled hat,
satin shoes. She holds my hand
and won't let go.

These are her socks.
The nursing home marked
the soles in ink. When I put them on
her initials
spread out under my toes.

Like Mother, Thirty Years Before Her Death

I'm grateful when the young man arrives
in his green fleece jacket, stamping and saying, *it's cold*,
carrying his metal bucket and glue boards,
not because of the scratchings I've heard in the ceiling,
the real ones, but because of the scratchings
I don't describe: the long stretch of time without company;
the night that begins at 5 p.m., TV
flickering gray and boring; at my side, the shut book.
When I open the door to greet him,
I realize why my mother—the summer my father
traveled with his secretary, the one who would later
become his second wife—brewed coffee
for the workmen who dug up our streets for sewers,
making us modern, suburban, and why she carried the cups
out to them, sugar in a silver bowl, cream
in a pitcher, cookies or finger sandwiches and napkins.
The men would stop work and smile, wiping
their foreheads, buttoning their shirts. I'd watch my mother
in her thin body, housedress, apron, straw sandals
offering her gifts to them—men who didn't refuse
but drank her strong coffee in the noon heat. I wondered
if she was flirting, but warning the young man to be careful,
to watch himself in the junk-filled crawl space, then
waving good-bye to him from the doorway
as he drives away with his poisons and traps, I know
she was simply doing what I am—being careful
and friendly with the time I have left, more anxious now
to fill the space with something human,
some small connection, a kindness, a shared platitude
that nevertheless, in retrospect, might count for something.

The Brightest Star Is Home

Driving home tonight after a good dinner,
you call that bright star to the right of the moon

Venus, but I say it's so far away
it might as well be home—that place where I was a child

and Father and I walked in the yard
like you and I did this afternoon before the bookstore,

where we spent too much, and the restaurant.
He would part the spiny ferns, move aside the violet mushrooms

to show me where elves slept in the cupped hands
of hollyhock. That place

where Mother ironed in a mist of steam
or gardened in a green straw hat, the summer night

falling over me like one of her fragrant scarves,
stars punched out of the dark like the bright holes

we poked in jelly jar lids so fireflies could breathe.
That place where Disney beckoned

from the small-screen TV, the castle exploded
in black and white

and Mother and Dad laughed
with Ed Sullivan and Milton Berle

as if they were uncles from out of town.
And bedtime (like now, when you and I move

in our silent rituals) was God's time,
when He might take me or leave me, and my last words

were offered to the night light and the universe,
my parents' footfall carrying them away

as if anywhere they were without me
was another galaxy—like that bright star you named Venus,

but, driving through the dark tonight, I pretend
might be that lost place I once called home.

Voices of Desire

There is no riddle like the twists of the heart; who shall
master them?

—Jer 17:9-10 (Knox Bible)

The bell ringing in your throat will drown
out the train's slow grieving.

—Anya Krugovoy Silver

Details of Flesh

That morning I surprised a nurse
and her patient, the two of them
together, bloodless skin and white
uniform like a shroud, but her hair,

it was black and crackling.
Then the sunburned neurologist
stripped an unconscious girl.
Let's see if she responds.

He rolled her nipple hard
between his fingers. Her body
arched, her breasts amazed.
So later, when the new doctor

found me alone in the room,
my white uniform neon
under fluorescent tubes,
I said *yes*. His tongue was salty,

his hands cold. I tasted his skin
clammy with so many bodies,
and I thought of them, my washcloth
making their skin gather,

the stark light on the details
of flesh. That day, in every ward,
nurses dripped lotion into their cupped hands,
and restless patients called them.

Hooked Up

Drunk, partying, she
and the man just hooked up
she tells me, the college student, the nervous
can't-sit-still woman,
dark-haired, laughing, pierced tongue,
pierced navel, colored threads
braided into bracelets around her wrist,
barely making it through finals,
graduating next spring then
maybe a job, but for today,
she says, the problem is fear,
what if I caught something, this worry
hooked into her and now
she slides down, eager but not eager
for me to do cultures, blood tests,
to tell her everything is fine.
Oh how often I've seen this,
this dread twisted in as if there might be
a tangle inside, shiny, metallic,
like wire, and how each time
I have to pull fear out,
strand by strand,
trying not to weep over this
one more woman hooked up,
these barbs deep into flesh,
and how they can only be extracted
with moans and cries, each one
ripping through until
there is no more innocence,
only this woman and me,
helpless to do anything

but go on pulling the hooks from her,
stuffing them into the garbage,
telling her how sweet it must have seemed
that night, how strong
she must be now, how resolute.

It Was a Good Year for Dreams

It was a good year for dreams. They came
    like poems and taught me.
    Everyone was there, especially
    my children. Kittens spilled
    into stairwells like buttons
    and men followed me, shadows
    darting past locked windows—
    the long "I" that knocks,
    knocks at the door. How to
    escape myself was the question.
    How to dream of Kandahar,
    Kosovo, even Turkey where
    a woman came out of the ruins
    in Ephesus, near the library,
    where Saint Sophia stands, frozen.
    You could see through the walls
    and the books were dust. She
    was our guide—bleached hair,
    a taste for American videos.
    She showed me her bruised eye,
    the red mark across her cheek.
    You must get away, I said when we
    kissed good-bye. It was a hot
    day, sweat like blood, my lips
    like the salty slap of a hand,
first on one side of her face, then on the other.

Young Woman on a Precipice

after Stars, *a painting by Maxfield Parrish*

The stars are infinitely joyful—
my hair, yellow as finches
and tied in a single plait,
awakens my back.

The rock is slag beneath me.
The air, like frayed silver cord,
investigates the spaces
between my toes.
My breasts and my belly are fresh,
and my thighs. Around me,

night is falling.
(This is the Grand Canyon or else
a dream. Below there is blue air, a darker rim
suggesting land.)

If I keep my balance on the precipice,
if I close my eyes,
the night will make love to me.
I am not afraid of her tongue or her breath,
small breeze that lifts the curtain

in a room where, as a child, I slept.
Hear it? Her laughter in my ear?
Stars were drawn through on a needle of light then,
and the moon with her curved back
rose from the abyss.

Ritual Bath

Steam-laden air and the summer night's heat
met and rose over us, mother and I adrift
on that Saturday night in Pittsburgh.
Ivory soap globes burst with a small

sting and ping, like seconds ticked away
by the Baby Ben on her bedside stand.
We bathed without speaking.
My fingerpads became old. Her breasts

rested sleepy on the meniscus of the water;
flakes of our skin made a ring
on the surface. The cloth was rough.
Heat lightning from a distant town

flared in the high bathroom window,
and the slippery curve of mother
rounded into pale fuchsia nipples
color of lips, of tongues, of the damask

rose towel slung on the door hook.
I gathered armfuls of soapsuds,
prisms that held mother's many faces
shimmering like fish roe—faces released

like a handful of new, glittering fish.
She plucked the stopper.
The water, sluicing down the dark
hatched mouth, left soap-foam clinging

to my chest, my own erect goosebumps.
Mother, suddenly cold, shivered and rose
from the boil of heat, a woman
rushing to her damask towel.

March 28, 2001 / March 28, 1945

I'm in my basement exercising when
the radio announcer says that on this
day in 1945, it was an unprecedented
eighty degrees. It takes me a moment
to realize that, fifty-five years ago,
my mother was twelve weeks pregnant
with me. Maybe she didn't know or
maybe she blamed the heat, oppressive
at the Maryland shore where she walked
with friends along the water's edge
trying to forget the war: my mother—
thin legs, flat breasts, brown hair,
blue eyes. Pausing now in my
basement, I feel her slight nausea, how
sweat trickles between her breasts
and dampens the underside of her hair.
My father's in Italy, every day he writes
her love letters from the Po Valley,
unaware that I have stolen part of them
both and come to life, a fish-like curl
in her uterus, a foreign body
that primes her ovaries, her estrogen,
progesterone, prolactin, the hormones
that make her, this very day, feel slightly
faint. She wades into the still-cold waves
and sits down there, splashing herself
with one hand, acclimating her skin
to the sudden chill. In Italy, my sun-
burned father sweeps land mines from
green depressions between the Apennines.
At night, he drinks wine and writes letters
before his turn at watch. This is the day

after his battalion entered Tezze,
triumphant, months before he'll win the
bronze star and come home half crazy.
Mother can't know that soon my body
will tear itself from hers and she'll birth
me at midnight, lightning stuttering the
labor room windows, an odd beginning
to the odd ending neither of us expects
when, at last no longer knowing who
I am, she will refuse my hand. When
she leaves the shore, suit damp to her
belly, when she hurries home to write
my father about how it was eighty
degrees so she went to the beach,
is she already unhappy or have I been,
all this time, mistaken? If only I could
ask what she hopes for, what she will
expect of me, and if she thinks, in any
way or at any time, I might ever please her.

Lot's Wife

Once she turned into salt,
good things happened. First she
was licked by doves, their little
tongues streaking her thighs.

Then, rain drizzled down.
She forgot the old story,
peaked like a breast, crystallized
like stars on the sand.

The wind blew in from Zoar.
Salt, she was happily invisible
and so scattered like dust.
She flew to her husband's iris,

gouging the cornea,
blinding the brown rind of his eye.

Partial Detachment

The Sunday morning after, fog outside
in the tree limbs like a premonition of snow,

he lies back, just awakened, elbows bent under his head—not
drawing away, but not yielding either. When I sit, the mattress

tilts slightly and his neck tenses. *How is it today*, I ask, and he shrugs,
blinks a few times, looks out at the deck

blurry with leaves.
Still a lot of floaters. He raises his hand to cover one eye,

then the bad eye. Moves his finger
tracking the amorphous blobs. Yesterday, when the retina

tore, he saw dark spiders he tried to smash on the wall.
Lucky, the doctor said. *Only a partial detachment.*

A few hours more and the vitreous might burrow under,
dissolve the retina's glue. Then he aimed the laser gun, *bam bam*

bam bam it fired green, noisy. That night,
his eye squinched like a boy who survives his first fist fight,

my husband couldn't get warm.
When he realized he could go blind, he made love to me,

his face in my collarbone.
This morning, drizzled tree trunks and bright leaves look

like they do reflected in water.
His eyes are so brown I have to imagine the pupil,

and beyond the surface find
the gelatinous chamber where vision occurs and the soul looks out.

He explains it to me: *Invisible nerves carry images to our brains,
but our brains fool us. How do we really know what's out there?*

You mean like Plato, I say, *the thing and the idea of the thing?*
His hands rest at his sides. *No*, he says, *that's not it.*

Late Afternoon Nap

Our eyes are closed
and our limbs abandon their poses.
Like animals at night,
we hope all hunters are lost,
all predators too full to bother.
When our hands twitch
or we rouse and doze again,
it is only the vestige of daytime,
how we don't dare speak of love.

Trees gather their shadows,
tap on our impenetrable window
as we slip deeper within ourselves,
unwilling to wake to the cold bite
of bedroom air, the glove of light
on our sleep-bloated faces.

You sit up and fumble for the clock.
I slip on my jeans and shirt.
Soon the owl will be out
swooping her silent executions
while mice and rabbits fret in their thickets—
not hopeless or angry, only wary
of sounds, of the wind changing course,
disturbing, again and again,
their ragged sleep.

Almost Fifty

at Martha's Vineyard

My husband sleeps. At noon, I creep
out to the summer shower on the deck,
one towel around my body, one
tossed over the wooden door. A red bi-plane
rising from Katama drones. Sun pours
silver from the shower head. I see
my body flawed, a shadow on the wall,
and close my eyes. A breeze stirs. A wren
repeats its five-note trill, cleaving my life
like lightning once split gray Waskosim's Rock
and left a fissure where we tried to hide.
Death is in the meadow and the fields.
The sky dark blue, I stand, struck blind.

The Jar beside the Bed

My partner, a man I didn't know before,
has dark hair and rarely speaks.
Now and then—and this was difficult at first—
we have sex, like animals, without love,
although we've become adept.
A woman watches us, as if we were
her pets. She keeps us here.

It's like a dollhouse, but we're not dolls.
We have a bed, a spare table and two chairs,
a table lamp. No books, nothing to entertain
except each other, which is, apparently,
how she thinks it ought to be.

She turns over in her bed to watch,
tings her nail against the glass as if we could be
fish, or monkeys in some Lilliputian zoo.
I have no memory of being captured,
or how I grew so small.

For fun, we mock her—
make up her name, or where she works,
or who she loves. She never says a word,
just stares, somehow
happier. It's an odd situation all around.

We have no calendar, no idea of time.
My hair's uncombed, grown long, and in the heat
sticks to skin, mine and his. Even our features,
I've noticed, have grown alike. We've become confused.

Here's the funny thing—
we don't look for weak spots in the jar.
We never think *escape*.
We never say *next week* or *yesterday*,
or try to shout for help when she's not home.

Instead, we pace the circle of our room
like hands around a clock.
We pick our skin. Occasionally,
we kiss or snarl like dogs. It's my job
to clean the inside of the jar.

Observed, observing, we stay
exactly as we are.

Leaving the Aquarium

The cement castle in the big tank
wavers in our gaze. We are weighted
to the spot. Overhead, a bulb shines
its sun-column through waves

pulsed from air jets. The water sings
and fish come to us
in all their costumes: *ragged man*,
trailing filaments of flesh like a torn shirt;

ugly face, gray lips rolled back;
scaredy-cat, suddenly inflating
to transparency; and *neon-darts*,
flashes of foil tucked in the grottos.

I tap good-bye on the silent glass,
wishing I could slip through water,
be silk-skinned without words or hours,
only melody and the slow circle.

Outside, a fine rain falls like ash,
turns to steam where heat-pumps vent
in the alley. We talk about dinner
and the seals with their sad-dog faces—

the children liked them best. Our car
moves as quietly as the shark that skims
the surface with his brothers. The water
streams in their wake; sheets of rain

sluice from our car. There are places
we cannot enter / times we cannot escape.
Like an emerald fish, I press my face
to the glass, tasting the metal edge.

Shipwrecked

The first few days we worked—
a lean-to, perpetual fire,
a makeshift tub. At night,

we told stories, and daytime we'd explore
the small island:
mostly forest with a beach

we walked daily, picking shells.
Monkeys stared, and fish
tempted us. We ate like cannibals,

discussed fidelity, truth. I let him
wash my back and braid my hair;
we became more lost.

We'd sleep until the sun went down,
then do Romeo and Juliet,
inventing swords, elaborate balconies.

I recited the nurse's speech;
fiddler crabs rushed beneath the moon.
A month went by.

You say you'd have good intentions?
At first we exercised, dried sponges for our bath,
tried to name the stars.

But we had no books, our memories were weak.
I invented *watch*. He liked
to watch me walk naked in the sea

and toss my hair. I watched him
pluck his beard.
When smoke marked a ship miles away,

he yanked me by the arm.
We pulled down our shack, then
he lay on top of me. We stayed like that

for hours. After dark,
I watched him fish, casting
on his belly in case the ship could see.

That night we ate in silence,
then played *fight*, his game, in which
we'd scream into each other's faces,

then make love, sobbing,
on the beach. The next morning
I began to keep a diary.

To the Husband Who Stands at the Sink, Intent on Shaving

There is a woman in your shower,
her body visible through the green
canopy of steam. Her dark hair
cleaves to her neck like leaves
and beads of water decorate her skin,
slide opal and diamond bracelets down
the blood flush raised by heat.
Every day she walks or lifts weights,
praising the way thighs tighten,
how muscles rise and divide her back
into twin slices of fruit—sweet,
succulent, firm against the lip.
Now she admires the long arm she raises
to direct the spray against her breasts.
Have you looked away from the mirror
to watch? In case you have, she turns,
giving you freely her profile, this map
of the body complete with betrayals
slightly hidden behind the wavering glass.
One hand ringed in gold slowly
approaches the faucet. Languid,
wide-awake, she prepares to emerge
like a water bird slipping from water
into air, feathers slicked, stripped clean
of anger and sorrow, not yet of expectation.

Voices of Suffering

At my wit's end
And all resources gone, I lie here,
All my body tense to the touch of fear.

—Elizabeth Jennings

Every happiness is a bright ray between shadows.

—Geraldine Brooks

Suffering

I.

In intensive care,
these sufferings:

a baby whose father had taken him
by both legs, a finger between them,

and hit the baby against the wall
because the baby cried. With the other hand

he held the mother back. A boy
fell off his bike and was hit by a car.

His mother watched him lying
in the clean sheets, his heart

beating under his chest
as if an animal were trying to escape.

The monitor line straightened;
then she howled for him.

There was a child who drowned
and a crazy woman we tied to the mattress

who rose up
with the mattress still on her back.

Once a man ran naked down the back stairs
into the parking lot

just to feel for the last time
the hard diamonds of snow.

II.

I've seen women
who were beaten

by other women
with a shoe, a stick, a picture frame.
A mother hits
the side of her daughter's face
with a flashlight.

Fathers use their hands,
to women mostly,
to their children
maybe something else.

One woman told me it wasn't the blows
but the love lost,
gone as if they peeled your skin,
sucked all marrow from your bones and now
you walk everywhere hollow.

III.

This is their sound.

It starts as a whine,
like a child's whine
when they can't have

what they want;

then it becomes
a staccato rap
finding your pulse;

then
intermittent,

like the high sound
when intestines churn,
trying to find something left
to pass through;

then it becomes
all there is,
small and pure,
a delicious drop
balanced on the tongue
of the open mouth;
then,
      Silence.

The Nurse's Task

When I pluck the suture
or pack the ulcer with gauze,
it becomes my task
to introduce rage to this body

that calls me, *nurse, nurse,*
as if my hands were gold.
First I cradle the body
like a mother rocks.

I lean close
and let it memorize my face.
Then, I begin.
First, something subtle.

A hasty scrape.
An accidental pinch
as if I might thrust needle
down to bone. The body

raises its hands in disbelief!
This is nothing. I thread veins
with catheters of fire,
I change morphine to milk.

When the body asks *why?*
I am silent. When the body
whines, I act bored
and turn away. If sleep comes

I sneak in and shake the body

until, angry and squinty-eyed,
it rises on its elbow
and stares at me, at last understanding

that the flesh is everything.
This is the body I love—the one
that laughs down death's trumpet.
The one that escapes.

To the Mother of the Burned Children

When you ask, when your voice
is your own again, and you know
you're not waking from sleep
or a vision of kids napping,
the power gone, candles
shaking light across their faces,
I'll give it to you straight:
Your children are dead.

You can cry one long sound
and we'll let the bed quake,
the burned flesh fall away.
I could bring shots to lull you,
pills to stay your mourning,
but instead I'll tell you:
Walk the fire in your mind.
Carry them out, one by one,
through rooms thick with smoke.
Carry your children, then put them down
safe outside the ring of heat.

Call them by name:
Ramon.   Priss.   Jamal.

Tell them, *Wait.*
Wait here. Wait.

Falling Temperature

The temperature is falling,
the first storm this winter due tomorrow
after months of unexpected warmth, but driving home

I think of temperature, and how
it climbs higher than you'd think, the human tongue
a bed of coals.

Frosty and mechanical,
we wrap patients in sheets of ice to keep
their brains from cooking. Fevers

plunge fast or else creep down
so slowly we can't save the memory,
then patients wake, confused.

Even our words
are hot: *crisis, defervescence, hyperthermia.*
We know the ache

behind their eyes, how they flush
and feel a desert in their veins, believing they might
burn like paper.

Better off dead, a woman told me,
a tumor in her hypothalamus, a funny word
that made me think of hippos

wading in the Amazon.
Her skin grew thick, the tumor igniting every cell
until she simply fried.

Crispy Critters—that's what nurses call
the burned kids, their bodies hot,
their skin so pink and thin

you want to prick them with a needle,
let some steam escape. Instead,
we peel their flesh

and wrap them tight in gauze
until their body heat drops too low
to register. Like tonight, driving home,

when, they say, the temperature is sure to fall.
I remind myself that they mean weather.
Weather, I say out loud. That's all.

Visiting the Lightning Struck

Imagine Moses, his tablets burned by God.
Or is this nature's wrath?—a man
whose skin is charred with ragged wounds
where bolts raged, piercing heart and lung.

No holy, dead-aimed stroke,
this summer lightning flash fired his corneas
to opaque glass and burst
his eardrums as if they were balloons.

Did fear come with, before, or after?
And did he see, or simply feel, bones smoke,
eyelids fuse? When his heart stopped,
did he gasp and wait until the tick resumed,

or did the lungs freeze first, then
the other organs fail? How will he think
of picnics after this, how love
August's hazy light, where bees drone air

thick as saturated gauze—until clouds
swell, random ions shift and currents
surge to kiss the ground? They say
he throws off blankets, wants all curtains

drawn. I smell his burns across the hall.
I say his name. I knock upon his door.

Distracted by Blackberries

I am distracted by blackberries, how suddenly I see them
in the bowl on the counter, black and shiny,
their little lobules like so many ants, a gang of them,
oddly quiet, at the same time quite alive, plump and taut,
as if touching the skin of a blackberry might rupture it,
the juices escaping. And don't they seem a bit ominous?—
how dark, how still, how like a small, burnt organ,
perhaps a brain pried from some charred body,
the *sulcus centralis* still precisely delineated, as if flames
only singed but did not destroy. I am distracted by blackberries
at the approach of autumn, its various anniversaries
of death. So I hold this little not-burnt, not-ant thing,
this glossy frightening blackberry, and decide not to eat it,
not to ingest all the smoke and fire of memory.

Hemorrhage, 3 a.m.

A boy walks into the sea.
Content at first, he floats
in the trivial current,
paddles like a dog.
Drifting, he streams
through a cold spot. His legs
cool, his arm hairs stand up,
making him laugh.
Now he's moving.

White caps peak and dip.
He thinks he could swim to shore
like a hero.

If he stops, his arms and legs
splay out and he's pulled along.
When the sea rocks, he rocks,
one with the onward rush.

Now he's moving.

He tries to speak and blood
tongues his throat.
He remembers how his mother lifted him
from the tub, enclosed him in a towel.
He thinks of smacking baseballs
with a wooden bat.

When he goes under
his hair circles and he sees it
as if he is above himself.

He's a boy-fish
moving with the tide
like a bullet, like a shark.

He thinks he'll wash ashore
and eat the children.
His body elongates.
Gulls would mistake him
for a woman's scarf trailed from a boat
or a kite tail
looping in the wind.

Far off, children play
in bright suits. The beach
is crowded with mothers.

> He turns into a ripple,
>> a crease in the surface of the sea.

Angel of Mercy

She has seen the artificial eye afloat in a glass,
and the wig in the bald lady's room. Undisturbed,

she directs her flashlight beam onto each sleeping face.
Patients twitch or feel a breeze. If they wake, they find an empty room,

bland curtains hanging, nurses' voices like a mother's distant song.
The Angel is busy checking, tucking.

She wipes her hands on her skirts, enters the room of her favorite,
the boy spun like a chrysalis in cocoons of tubes and stainless wires.

He drifts to the blink-tap of pumps, the syncope of bellows.
He dreams he is face up in a rowboat, her light a single, red sun

wormed through his lids. She bends to kiss his lips,
her lips dry as wool, then she plucks him from his tethers,

hoists him like a sack. He dreams his boat is rocked by waves.
Tubes snap. Blood sprays the ceiling. The monitor goes blind.

Doctors hurry into the room, flail the boy until he is blue and marbled
and they are spent. They cover the shell of his face.

Down the hall, limping, out of breath, the Angel runs, her favorite
dancing on her back like awkward wings.

Patient in Surgery, 7 a.m.

Dazed by the needle's punch,
she sees faces ooze into spotlights,
the staff, hooded and slow,
bent to their tasks like aliens.

She never knows
if she's awake or sleeping—
only that her mind swells,
a merry-go-round begins
and she rides the rise and fall
of black rubber and stainless steel.

They told her she wouldn't dream,
but she runs naked in the body of her youth
while men shout some foreign language
she forgets at once. She wakes
screaming with her mouth shut.

She raised six kids, had a man once
whose body cleaved hers
like a blade splits an apple.
When he left, she wore her knees down
scrubbing other women's floors.

New sutures draw the edges
of her wounds tight; she wonders
how long silk can hold. Later
she tells everyone how the knife
went in before she was ready.

The Barking Dog

There is a woman
in a hospital
barking like a dog.
The nurses know
it's the sound
of her lungs going
and her heart.
Visitors think
it's a dog outside
chained to a tree,
the rope too short,
no water,
no one passing by.
All day and all night
visitors worry.
Why doesn't someone
bring in that dog?
People give the dog
names, people ask
if anyone can see the dog
through the window.
When the barking stops
everyone is relieved.
Elaborate endings are told—
how the dog
was taken to a farm
and set free.
How the dog
drinks from a stream
whenever it wants.
The nurses

say nothing.
But every nurse knows
the story
of the barking dog.

A Patient Tells about Her Suffering

— at first, it was a nagging in her throat,
a cough that stirred itself like a drowsy animal.

For days she went to work, dragged herself around,
went home early. But always, the body is inventive—

soon it became an animal enraged.
Muscles on fire, she felt the room

dipping and rising like a country road.
Nights brought on depression,

a certain desperation, a transparency of flesh
that almost seemed a gift,

something she might dedicate.
And so, she said, she offered every ache, each sleepless hour,

and when her illness seemed to worsen,
she listed all the things she'd done or failed to do.

At last, healing came.
Isn't it odd, she asked, *how long the nights can seem,*

everyone asleep, only the cold outside and your thoughts,
like owls,

sweeping through the woods on the urgent
down stroke of their wings?

I'm Afraid of the Brief Empty Space

I'm afraid of the waiting room where patients wear slacks and slip-off shoes
and families read last month's magazines;

of the aide who calls my name, staccato and without love,
who walks before me down the long hall, never looking back.

I'm afraid of the johnny coat—its cold exposure—and of the black tubing
looped on the wall and the clear tubing hooked to the oxygen tank;

of the nurse who comes with her IV bag and hollow needle,
asking my name and why I'm here, as if she doesn't know.

I'm afraid of the orderly who arrives with a wheelchair to roll me away,
of the white room and the scrub tech busy with her Mayo tray of shiny tools;

of the doctor who waves to me from the scrub room, his mouth
moving under his mask, and of the circulating nurse whose eyes say nothing.

I'm afraid of the brief empty space, the metal taste, the ringing in my ears
and the utter blackness into which I fall and do not know I'm falling.

I'm afraid of waking in the tilting room, of the circle of curtains
and the microphone voice of the nurse who calls my name;

of her snack of Ginger-ale and crackers—one fizzes too loudly,
the other breaks with the sound of bone and scatters over my body.

I'm afraid of the long wait for pathology, for the prognosis and how
at home when the doctor phones, he asks first how I feel, then if I'm alone—

Becoming the Patient

1.

In the hospital, after the operation
when the clear tube that drained my stomach
felt like fire in my throat
and the intravenous pinched my skin
I saw, like a waking-up dream, a nurse leaning over me
her arm so close all I could see were the blonde hairs
and the glistening gold of the bracelet at her wrist
and in that second I thanked God for the beauty
of the bracelet and the arm
that offered the scent of soap
and for the silent tending all those nights
when all I could see was the arm, that glittering gold
even in the dark when drains were emptied
and oxygen adjusted it was that arm and that
delicate strand
that held me to my life

2.

In the hospital, in the haze of could-die
could-get-better
I came to understand gender
not in the way I'd always thought
male and female
the externals and the assumed
but in how it was sometimes the feminine
my body sought
and other times the masculine

how necessary both
the tender gentle sympathy
and other times
the strength and deference
that lifted and held and did not let me fall

3.

In the hospital when the fever would not go down
and fluid seeped from my veins to swell my skin
when lungs filled with water
and infection devoured muscle and blood
when they offered protein in yellow IVs
and blood in bright red bags
when the blood poured in poured out again
and every breath threatened me
when the CT scan whirred and the machines pinged
and not one test came to my defense
when God abandoned me in the second week
and only the dark night sky looked in
when I thought I could die I told myself
and told myself that there were others who suffered
and others who were whole

4.

In the hospital every morning the surgical residents
came by at 5 a.m., blazing on the lights
and standing around the foot of my bed
five or six of them, a nightmare of women and men
asking *how do you feel this morning*
not waiting for my reply but rather

descending upon my body
one listening to my heart and another
pushing my belly, lifting the bandages and
shaking the drainage bag and two others
at my legs, pressing skin to bone to see how much
edema remained, pressing and pressing
until I said *stop* and no one knew which one
was hurting me, the belly or the legs
and once when I began to retch the chief resident
said she'll be fine and as he led them away
each one smacked the hand sanitizer device
on the wall to release the purifying gel
rubbed their hands once or twice
and went on to the next patient

5.

In the hospital my husband stayed
he stayed by my side
when I woke from one surgery and then another
he stayed
when they drew my blood and changed my tubes
when I peed or filled the commode with blood
when I cried he stayed
he didn't leave when I retched
and if I walked he walked with me
gathering my IV lines and holding my arm
if I slept he sat in the corner and waited
when I was in pain he stayed
he stayed after visiting hours were over
and he arrived before they began
when God abandoned me
my husband stayed

when nurses changed shifts
or doctors debated what to do next
when tests couldn't be done until midnight
my husband stayed
when I was in the hospital
my husband stayed

6.

In the hospital the third week
the nurses took pity, moved me to the best room
the executive suite with built-in bookcases
a private shower, a DVD player
with stacks of movies, mostly comedies
and a large TV that hovered over the foot of my bed
staring at me
while in its face I watched the sky's reflection
and yet the machines still hissed and pinged
IVs still pinched
the elderly women in the next room
cried *help me help me* all night long
and the fluid in my lung became a rising tide
when the doctor drew the fluid out
with a long needle of pain
the specimen was overlooked in the lab
the test ruined
and my fancy room didn't comfort me at all
it just lifted its haughty nose in the air

7.

In the hospital I waited all night

for medication to lull or exhaustion to overcome
but pain meds only made my mind hyper-aware
of the chatter of janitors on break
the hum of the family waiting room TV
bursts of laughter or voices that wafted by my room
and when a nurse flicked on the lights to check my vitals
hang a new IV or silence an alarm
I quietly offered my arm, my heart, my belly
and when she left
I watched the mute clock on the wall
and like all sleepless patients
I saw the phantom who waits until night
to seize the second hand
holding it back until the hours drag
in a slow and unremitting crawl

8.

In the hospital as soon as you can stand
you must walk, so I walked
tubes clamped and pinned to my robe
my IV stand a silver circle with four poles
each holding its own swaying bag
the yellow was my food, the red my blood
two for antibiotics, I'd push the rolling stand into the hall
surprised each time
by the hospital's vast bright life
nurses busy at their stations, residents with their laptops
only the cleaning lady a silent presence
who nodded as I crept by, not sure I'd make
the endless loop past the room with the ice machine
the sandwiches and pudding I could not eat
then down the long stretch where I'd pass other patients

on their daily stroll
and I could guess their illnesses
a man with prostate cancer, his crimson urine bag
the woman with breast cancer, her bald head and IV chemo
a young man, his tubes like mine
we didn't smile or stop to talk, too afraid
too eager to escape each other's sorrows
and lie down with our own

9.

In the hospital I learned
who I really am
in the midst of suffering I saw
my faults, my lack of faith
I kept notes at my bedside
in an almost unreadable hand
how often I have failed to care for others
what do you do when nothing is left
when you are emptied
when my suffering is relieved I feel no joy
is this despair
if I am to die, may I die soon
suffering has exposed me: intolerant
confused, selfish, unloving
there is nothing that cheers me
is suffering prior to death required
am I being punished
what does my suffering teach others
have I not said thank you enough
what does God want of me
have I totally misunderstood

10.

In the hospital after twenty-six days
I was released
it took hours for the order to be entered
for my nurse to come back from the office
where she was, that very morning, let go
part of a general lay off
she told me as she removed my IV
and tried not to weep
what would I do without her
without Sarah, Debbie, Jeanette, Alex, Elsa,
Ana, Leslie, and Miguel, who'd survived Iraq
and held me when I couldn't hold myself
without Jessica and Josyane, who wasn't afraid
to get wet when she bathed me as I stood naked
in the bathroom, who changed my sheets
more often than the rules allowed
I didn't know how I would survive at home
until the just-let-go nurse embraced me
and sickness became a place I left

The Ant's Reprieve

Last night I noticed an ant in the shower stall
and decided not to kill it.

By morning, I had forgotten, turned
on the water and stepped in.
A moment later, a scalded black bead
circled the drain.

But, I had spared the ant before,
giving it eight, ten more hours—time
for several dreams!

What benevolent, careless eye
watches me, now?

Voices of Faith

If 'ecstasy' meant the sudden intrusion of the sacred into the
ordinary,
then it had just happened to me.

—Abraham Verghese

—the meeting place of Heaven and Earth
has always been the human body, quietly.

—Dick Allen

The Vocation of Illness

Today, when he speaks about holiness, the priest says
that some people have the vocation of illness. I think about this

all the way home, the gray-spired church growing smaller
in my rear view mirror, and the vocation of illness looming

before me like a re-run movie, like when I was a new nurse
at St. Joseph's and my first patient was a woman

dying of a brain tumor, before all the sweet nectars of relief
we have today, before the precise knife and bitter healing poisons.

I stood beside her bed as she writhed and groaned,
the harsh white sheets tossed and tugged into disarray.

As I straightened them, as I offered water, company, a back rub,
I'd listen to her constant moan, a long low sound

that rose into a shriek and then receded, like a fierce surf
that roiled and thundered in, then hissed back into the endless,

deepest, darkest blue. When I worked the night shift, I'd find her
still awake, eyes wide, voice hoarse from constant keening.

And today, after all this time, I learn that she was holy,
immolated on a cross I couldn't see. *Hello, woman who died in agony.*

Can you hear me? Have your cries turned to singing?
Do you stand before the face of God?

The Next Word You Say

might be the name of God.
Dragonfly. Orange.

A nervous bug
with mylar wings thin as mother's net

over a fruit bowl in 1955.
When I poked the orange with my thumb

the *niebla de zumo* stung my eyes. *Ice cube.*
Grosbeak. Tongue. Outside, crows

puff up their bodies. Can you trust
the next word that comes to you?

Monkey, lily, windmill.
And if so, how exactly will you know?

(*niebla de zumo:* "juice mist"—the fragrant mist
that spritzes up when you cut or tear an orange)

Then It Was Simple

You walked up Sylvandell Drive
on the coldest night. Soon, Father would be home,

easing the gray Plymouth into the one-car garage,
and Mother, who was always home,

would be cooking meatloaf with its two
sizzling strips of bacon. Snow stung your face,

snow crunched beneath your boots and the glow
from Pittsburgh's steel mills hung in the sky.

In such a place, Mary could appear to you
casually, leaning out the neighbor's window,

a blue domestic angel with a movie star face,
round arms crossed on the sill, her brown hair

in a friendly page boy. She smiled, you smiled back,
your sled tugging behind you,

grounding you, and the frozen snow and the whirl of gravity
holding you, and Mary,

as if she were not from another world,
so happy to see you.

On the Radio

I'm driving, listening to the news,
the evening punctuated
by neighbor's Christmas lights and by stars,
when from behind the announcer's voice
comes a child's voice singing.

> *I remember windows*
> *higher than my head, curtains*
> *made of lace. Our yard, ice covered,*
> *sloping down to Wightman Street.*

I turn the radio up, then down,
trying to get the voice in clear: a child
singing in a room, alone.

> *Mother had just been there with me,*
> *watching as cars skidded down our hill.*
> *She let the curtain fall and walked away.*

The child's voice fades in and out.
I watch the road, twist the dial.

> *The house was warm, and God had been*
> *in all my mother's tales, in all*
> *the glitter-covered cards. From the kitchen,*

On the sidewalk, a man
stops to light a cigarette. The match
flares—the child disappears.

> *I heard a carol on the radio,*
> *and so began to sing.*

At The Bedside of the Dying

for my father

1.

The box that held your ashes was square and bulky.
When I touched it, it felt as if you burned inside, the energy
released from your body
like the white hot creation of a star.
A man lowered the box
and it fit neatly into your grave,
settled with a sound like the sigh you made
when the internist said *malignancy* and, finally,
when the time came not to mince words,
the cancer's spread.

When I review our last hours together,
I number my errors, like doctors who, after the harm is done,
dissect a troubling case. How difficult it is,
how necessary, to stay at the bedside of the dying.

2.

I didn't hold your hand enough, or read to you,
or recount the ways I loved you.
I didn't let my face glow with gratitude or pale into sorrow
but instead turned to you with our perpetual family smile.
Once, when you asked if humans could express what was inexpressible,
I said it didn't matter.

I stroked your forehead, the moist beads slicking your scalp,

the many imperfections of your aged skin, rosettes and decorations,
and I met your gaze at the moment of your going, of your brilliant
scrutiny—I wonder if you could hear my repeated *I love you*,
your hearing aide plucked out because it was whistling,
my voice, calling you, like a child's voice, urgent and high.

3.

After your lungs stopped,
after your eyes clouded and sank, after I hushed my fingers
over your eyelids and they closed as easily as they do in the movies,

after the hospice nurse came and pronounced you dead
and the aide came to wash you,
I had to get away from your empty shell
and the closed bedroom curtains to the living room

where you'd packed a cardboard box
labeled "What's left of my life."
When the hearse arrived and a man in a somber suit
carted your body off on a covered gurney,

I hid in the kitchen, out of sight. Near me,
your desk and chair, your typewriter and the file cabinet,
marked with a parable to guide me: "This drawer won't open
unless the other drawers are closed."

4.

I helped your wife change the damp sheets
on the bed where I'd kept vigil beside you the night before,

listening to the hiss of oxygen and the drone of summer rain, and before I left, I ransacked the house like a thief,

taking everything,
releasing you from that life and from me

into everything inexpressible,
into the luster and glory that now was yours.

Night Nurse

behold, the angels of God
            —Genesis 28:12

Angel,

hold their hands while I hurry
from patient to nameless patient,

feeling their skin beneath my hands
like tattered dresses stinking

of urine. Now they are sobbing.
Touch me! an old man says. *Touch me.*

The women want to steal my flesh.
They cry out, *Take my place!*

Angel, you go. Go into the corridors
where their bodies wither before me.

They die rolling in their beds,
they die sitting on their toilets.

When I try to give them breath,
their vomit comes into my mouth.

Angel,

when a patient's skin is moist with pain
and pain wakes him and sings him to sleep,

when a patient's family turns away
and his hands fall empty to the sheets,

then everything is multiplied.
A sip of cold water could be a thousand lakes;

a nurse appearing in the doorway
could be someone who loves him.

Angel, when their lungs stop and their eyes
slick over and stare, when their skin

purples from toe to thumb to hollow cheek,
you be the one who gentles the world;

you be the one who stays,
all these lives flying from us.

I Want To Work in a Hospital

where it's okay
to climb into bed with patients
and hold them—
pre-op, before they lose
their legs or breasts, or after,
to tell them
they are still whole.

Or post-partum,
when they have just returned
from that strange garden,
or when they are dying,
as if somehow because I stay
they are free to go.

I want the daylight
I walk out into
to become the flashlight they carry,
waving it
so God might find them
as we go together
into their long night.

God and the Blueberries

I selected the blueberries from the blue bowl left uncovered overnight in the refrigerator.

I felt the blueberries in the palm of my hand. They were small, like tiny eggs, but not like eggs. Some were soft and caved in, not quite rotten—like old men and women.

For a moment before releasing them, I wondered if blueberries knew about transformation. In the refrigerator, they had been safe.

I scattered the blueberries over my cereal. They fell into the milk, turning it blue like breast milk, and the blueberries became small blue breasts.

Outside, the sky was blue, and sugar turned red in maple leaves that soon would be brown as the stem hole of a blueberry.

I rolled the sweet blueberries from palm to fingertips and, one at a time, one at a time, they disappeared.

Rain Tree

for Nina

On Erev Rosh Hashanah the doctor gave you
a diagnosis, culled from the sticky cells
he pulled carefully from your brain. "The official name,
he said, "is glioblastoma." *Fuck statistics*, you said,
I'm going to dance at my niece's wedding.

All day it's rained. When I was a child I chose
a rain tree in every yard we moved to, a tree
visible from my bedroom window.
At night, rain glistened from the branches
like the Christmas icicles Mother taught me to drape,
carefully, a few strands at a time.

When I visit my mother's grave
I imagine her, head this way, feet over there.
Standing looking down, I force myself not to move,
daring her to thrust her arms up suddenly
and pull me under. Otherwise, I remember her
from photos, beautiful and thin.

Memories of rain trees, of how mothers look,
of how each birthday might be the last
gather tonight in dense, visible clouds—
and I walk through them.

Scattering Her Ashes

Let the day be warm and the sky in Rowayton be blue,
broken with clouds.

Let the bridge over the inlet be ours alone,
and let me recognize her son after all these years,
the boy I knew when his mother and I were best friends,
single mothers in nursing school.

Let us move to the railing, to the water, the marsh grasses
grown summer tall, shimmering in the sun.
Give us patience as we struggle to open the box
that holds her remains.

When the seal is broken, let us stand, leaning together,
arms linked. Let my prepared reading be insufficient;
let the paper be folded and replaced by tears.

Let us release her ashes in fistfuls; let her be caught
and lifted, a dance gritty and drifting.

Let me not flinch when she turns in the breeze,
touches my face, and I breathe her in.

Let me not despair when some ashes settle under the bridge,
caught on the metal edge, or when her ashes form a film
on the water's skim and float downstream.

Let me remember what we studied so long ago: How a nurse
might help the body live. And how, on the wards, we learned
to step aside—our hardest lesson—when to let the body die.

The Swan by the Mall

The swan's white bulk—crumbled like a corrugated box,
one white wing angled up like a broken fan—
rolls from side to side with the rush of passing cars.
I drive by, and as I do I see an angel rise from the swan's body,
hover briefly, then turn to look at me
as it opens its wings and circles like a helicopter.
When an angel rose from Joe Costanzo, the same joy
came over me. Joe had just exhaled that long
whoosh, the breath that emptied the lungs even before
the heart's last thump. As Joe's pulse leapt into the room,
I saw his pupils dim, like candles damped
with two moist fingers. It was a busy Wednesday,
nurses rushing about. Then the angel,
unfolding itself and blinking.
The rest of the shift, white gauze was tender
under my fingertips, and blood had the fragrance of peonies.
Other nurses nodded, each recalling her stories:
One angel spoke. Another stole a ring and hid it
in her pocket.
                        The swan disappears,
and I pull into the parking lot. Who wouldn't hurry
to the bedside of the dying, just to see the angel again as it goes,
drawing itself from death's shrunken belly into the room?

Snow Geese, Like Angels

In October, the snow geese return
to Cap Tourmente, having flown without rest
from the Arctic, where the females nested.
Now they preen their broken feathers,
grow fat on bulrush roots.
Eyes blank, heads thrust under a wing
or twisted back, they wonder where they are,
when they will be called.

One morning they rise up, brilliant
and crying, a white canopy
through which rain begins to fall.
Like angels, they do not sleep,
and they do not drink. Like saints,
they will die, lifting their wings to discover
wounds of red, like roses, tucked into flesh.

Absolution

Crows have been throwing themselves
at my windows for days. They stand on the deck,
crying, staring in as if they see something

I cannot. Then, feet first, bodies braced,
one by one, they hit and drop away,
scolding with thick tongues,

claws screeching the glass
like the scritch of chalk on a blackboard.
I leave corn and oats on the window sill,

scatter shiny foil and yarn as gifts in the grass.
There, I say, *I've given you everything.*
Still, crows circle the house in their capes,

glossy green in the sun, black caps pulled
over their nervous orange eyes.
Yesterday, I shouted to no one,

What is it? What do you want?
(That night I woke and watched you sleeping,
your strong jaw like a barrier.)

Once in a garden I saw a woman
lay down her purse and take off her shoes.
She pushed her open palms away,

as if disbelieving the roses.
Then she pulled the air around them to her,
as if inviting their spirit.

At day break, I stand in the reflection
of crows, open wide my arms.
Eager, forgiving, they enter me, and are gone.

Holy Thursday

The trees, bare black at winter's end, bow and wave
in my backyard like priests in their cassocks.

The rain pretends to be this evening's *asperges*,
and the grass bends in the wind the way the faithful genuflect

when the priest passes by with his censer, a little ripple
moving through the church like sunlight.

All day, I have waited in my room, watching out the window
for the Holy Ghost. I know he is there—

he could be the junco at the feeder or the gray dove
frightened in the driveway when the delivery man drove away.

I feel the Spirit hovering in the syntax of poems,
the suspension of activity, the held breath

of my long waiting.
Once I searched the Internet to find the saint most unlike me,

one I could pray to, follow around
like my daughter's chicks, newly hatched, follow her.

Ever since I was a child,
I wanted to spend my life in praise.

Instead, I eat breakfast and go to work,
lay hands on the sick, the mournful,

the mothers who sit before me,
ripe with new life or emptied by loss.

The lucky ones lift their newborns; I look into their eyes,
that blue gelatinous haze. Surely

the Holy Ghost is looking back
from those dark pupils. And yet, even now, at poem's end

the earth does not quake; the curtain, not yet torn,
does not shiver in the breeze.

Voices of Letting Go & Holding On

Deliver time and let it go
Under wild clouds and passive moon.

—Elizabeth Jennings

You have to keep breaking your heart until it opens.

—Rumi

Leopold's Maneuvers

the four maneuvers used by an examiner
to determine the lie of an unborn child

The belly an albino bowl
suddenly come to life, my hands
ready in the four positions
like the four witches in Oz
or the four winds that breathe,
all of us diviners. First
I cup the belly's pregnant curve
high under blue-veined breasts,
brim the slope and wiggle where an unborn
human head is round and hard,
the breech irregular. Second maneuver
and my palms embrace her sides, swelling
woman and curled child, where is your
back? Where are your small parts?
Third maneuver, my right hand grasps
the pubic hollow, fingers open
and close around the round ball
of a head, head ball, chin down, breech
balled at the fundus under
blue breasts, oblivious. And last,
great mother, as if compelled
toward the face of miracles,
my hands plunge the gutters
of a pelvic inlet I can only imagine,
feeling for the brow, the flexed
crown, the direction this child will take
emerging into light, our world,

this earth from its watery heaven
into its own brief span and back again,
      my hands
waving *hello, good-bye, hello, good-bye.*

Parturition

Coyotes quarrel with the Long Night Moon.
I'm young. My first child is due.

I can't sleep. Scorpions hurry
to hide in every crack. I worry—

will I be wiser than my parents?
Back home, my mother wakes,

her daughter's face
among dogs and rattlesnakes.

She writes me: *Scorpions invade my dreams.*
Are you in danger?

But I love the coyotes' dirge,
their hollow outline on the ridge,

and how the wild boar stink, wet with rain.
At 3 a.m., my labor pains begin.

Water Story

I love the living sound of my plant when I water it,
the hiss and suck of *agua*
pulled through the soil by gravity,
the sweat that appears on the clay pot,
the unwrinkling of the leaves.
I had a patient once, pregnant mother
morning sick and evening sick, who arrived
hauling her children, carrying her bucket.
We slipped a needle in her vein,
dripped saline into her body's dry core
and, right before me, the woman
plumped up. My ivy overflows—
a thread of water and fertilizer returns to earth
through the sink mouth. I am happy
that all life is circular. Seven months later,
the woman's chubby boy popped out, head first.
Blood and water flooded the catch basin, spilled over.
I carry this story on my white shoes.

On Not Loving Your Children

Stop loving them at two.
August nights, when rain comes in the window
and lightning snaps the air,
don't run to them.
Or, if you must, don't look into their eyes,
the clear glass of your own fear.

If you love them at ten,
turn away from baseball, dance class,
or the riding ring. Their slim bodies
split the air like fish.

By sixteen there is no hope.
They circle farther and farther away,
whistling to friends in strange tongues,
shining in skin you don't remember
touching or bathing.

At twenty, they are gone,
the air filled with their mist.
If you love them still, turn on your back,
stare into the sun for their reflections,
swirling and leaping like burning gases,
the sea-swell, the undertow.

She Opens a Book of Poems

She opens a book of poems,
pages she last read when married to her children's father.

The book becomes her recollection of him,
and she wonders if some skin cells remain on the pages,

cells cast off from his hand when he might have picked up the book,
curious to see what his wife was reading.

The turned pages become the years of their marriage,
the poems' uneven lines are her body and his body,

and the poems' metaphors might be their two children, facing her,
breathing accusations she can't deny.

She searches the spare couplets for forgiveness but instead
finds *lunch box* and *swaying trees* and *t-shirts bleaching on a clothesline,*

words as common as last month's electric bill
and as distant as that July when she took the children away,

their father standing alone in the parking lot, a place
unadorned and empty as the white space that hems in every poem.

Staring into the Point Where
the Tracks Merge

I am staring down the tracks
as if staring would bring the train,
as if staring would bring anything.
There is a long time for thinking
and something time does to thoughts,
compresses them, the rain and the moon
half-seen behind trees, a row of them
like silent women.

A man with a daughter joins me.
We all stand staring into the point
where the tracks merge.
We move our feet on the damp platform
watching our footprints appear,
lighten, and go back into wood.
I wonder about the man and his daughter.
Maybe someday he will fall in love

with a woman who is not her mother,
becoming hateful even to himself.
For now he is afraid that his child
stands too close, and he calls her back.
Then there is a silent time
when he thinks she is safe, and we wait,
satisfied with blue air
and the grace of tree limbs that rise
like women's hair into evening.

Ear Examined

The doctor tugs the fleshy lobe, pulls up
and back, the canal thereby made straight.
Enter his probing speculum, its light a triangle
on the drum. Pearly, uninformed, it waits
for the otoscope's puff of air. Like a sheet

snapped by tiny chambermaids, it flaps,
teased by air to test its worth for sound:
those words we long for—a whispered oath, a lie.
A trickster, the ear. Making us believe
what eyes deny or hearts might doubt,

the narrow bones inside like a sparrow's bones
in flight, willing to trust the slightest breeze,
the one that sings *Yes! I love you!*—
as if words might mean exactly what was heard.
Oh, the risk, the fragile wing.

Reading in Hayestown Elementary School
on Wednesday

In the hallway, Raeanna and I are enraptured
by words, alone in a universe we've devised,

her homeroom like a city across town
with its muffled chatter, muted sounds of scissors and chalk

and, once in a while, the call and response of the alphabet.
Raeanna's finger traces the page,

her lips expel the puff of air that means *p*
and then the funny, nasal *ony*—she says them together,

points to the shaggy pony in the book
and rides away, leaving behind her pink sweater,

the small oak chairs,
the white paste pots of third grade in Danbury.

I lean with her over the syllables,
learning the freedom of *run*, the beauty of *violet*

and *bread*, daring the uncertain, silent *k* in *know, knead,*
knock and, without warning, I see my mother,

just before she went blind, how she'd touch
everything, running her dry hands over my face,

reading the Braille of table tops with her fingerpads,
spidery, hesitant at first,

then expertly judging green or silk, even after
the macula failed, the eye's center closed.

Raeanna points to "snoozed" and asks,
like sleeping, right?—

as she maps out the future, her vision
unencumbered, and so earnest it could awaken the dead.

First Love

In July we danced in his garage
to *No Other Love Have I*, and after

I let him kiss me. We were awkward
as the dust-clotted rakes leaning

against cinderblock, perfect as the long days
of summer that hurled us into winter,

to the cold January night when I watched him
top the hill crest, his sled

scattering bits of light as it whooshed down,
the only other sounds the scrunch of snow,

the echo of someone's voice,
then the impact of an unseen car.

His body arched, silver and thin,
loosened and flung into snow.

A few lights appeared. Mothers and fathers
milled onto the road, then Denny's dad found him,

lifted him, and as he cradled his body
I remembered the scent of Denny's skin,

like sand in July. I never knew I loved him
until months later, I wrote *Denny* on my notebook

and said his name out loud. It wasn't exactly grief I felt,
but the sure, quick rush of life against the drag of time—

like the night Denny strung tin cans and string
from his house to mine. Leaning out our windows,

we talked, watching our breath puff
and fade, a slow arc that softened into dawn.

Everything in Life Is Divided

Everything in life is divided:
twenty-four hours that fade from day to night,

the sand at Martha's Vineyard, where we vacationed last year,
separating us from the ocean

where we swam, then returned to our blanket,
the two of us making one marriage,

sharing the apple sliced to reveal the identical
black seeds of its surprised face.

Even our bodies can be halved, although less evenly:
lungs partitioned into lobes, the heart's blood

pumped from right to left, the brain's two hemispheres
directing our arms, our legs,

our lives into the two possibilities of the Greek mask.
My life's work, too, is divided—

on one side of my desk, unfinished poems;
on the other, nursing books with dog-eared pages.

Aren't we all somehow divided?
Like when my daughter was in labor, my first

grandchild emerging into the room's blue air,
suddenly entering new territory,

and how, when after the delivery my daughter kept bleeding,
I couldn't look at the newborn in the incubator

but stood fast beside my child, the woman who once
slipped from my life into her own and now had divided herself again

while I balanced in my hands *Joy* and *Fear*, cradling them both
until the bleeding stopped.

How I Imagine It

Ahead of me on the road, my daughter
and her husband in their old Subaru.
He's driving and I'm following them to the Danbury garage
to fix the ping that's been there for weeks
when suddenly their car careens, crashes into a tree
and bursts into flames. I park my car, just stop it
and run, run to the door bashed off its frame.
My hands reach in, carefully,
across her silky printed dress, the white-collared one
she likes so much. She is thin
and graceful, I unhook her seat belt,
the silver metal clasp snaps open and the webbing falls away,
her head tilted as if she's sleeping,
but I smell gas, the stink of burning tires.
People cry out, shouting to me, *Get away!* I lean in,
incredibly strong, and lift her up and out,
she is all air, long arms, hands with my knucklebones.
I hold her, wrap her dress around her knees,
her husband lies over the steering wheel, the horn blasting,
like in the movies, and I run, holding her in my arms.
I kneel by the roadside, let her body unfold
in a tree's green shadow, into long stems that smell like cut grass
the summers my father pushed the handmower and mother
made lemonade, squeezing the lemons in her hands, picking
each seed out. I bend,
knowing if I can save her, I can save myself, if I save her
she will forgive me for everything I have ever done,
for everything I have allowed to be done. I bend
and place my mouth over hers, take in one big breath, breathe it
into her mouth, into lungs that catch, grab it,
hurl it through to her heart, her heart

holds and contracts, once, again, again and she gasps for air.
I feel her warm, every cell ignites and glows, she is
alive.... The light
turns yellow, turns red. Their car slows ahead of me, stops.
The stoplight swings in the wind. It's almost Autumn.

Dreaming for the Blind Goat

An infection, the vet said, fibrin and pus knit a blue cataract
and the goat trips through shadows, bleats at our voices,

nibbles our scent. We cup our hands to give her water.
My daughter strokes the nanny, feeds her crackers.

My own child, I've seen her in a dark room, naming
the stations of her life: father gone, first love failed, wanting mother.

Sometimes her eyes in the night
are black as the nanny's skin.

In the sweet air my lungs with their fine cords catch the purse
of my breath. I say, *we must trust that the blind goat dreams.*

My daughter closes her eyes.
An island of goats, she says, *a vision of goats ascending a mountain,*

calling out with voices like women, seeing themselves in the sky.
She believes love could draw stars from the night,

shadows disappearing in their glow. Her caring
holds more pain than can be put into time. Let me find the words;

let me take her hand. *Forgive me my own shallow*
and vacant eye. Let me hold you as you cry.

Moon Watching

for Chris

I woke you at midnight.
The TV was on, a bright flickering
in the living room. The men looked
like they were in a movie—thick arms and legs,
the same huge heads they had in *Captain Video*,
spaceship skidding, kicking up moon-dust.
I held you on my knee and pointed,
Look, Neil Armstrong walking on the moon!

You were barely one year old: part soil,
part blood, a bit of rain. Your sister ran
and placed her hand against the screen,
but you were bored. We watched until
the flag was raised, the famous phrase still new.
Then we called *goodnight moon,*
goodnight astronauts, and went to sleep.

Tonight, I drive away from your new house.
You stand, waving briefly, at the door,
your yard full of birch trees, your garden
sprouting new tomatoes in the dark.
The moon is almost full, its shadows
still the same. And here we are—
earth in our hands. Sky bringing rain.

It Was the Second Patient of the Day

It was the second patient of the day
whose arm reminded me of my daughter's arm,

and so I wanted to touch the firm flesh
along the ulnar ridge and the soft skin in the elbow's bend

and press my lips to the few freckles,
to the sweet and salt taste of my daughter.

Then it was the nape of a young man's neck,
how, when he turned away, a twin ridge of muscle

rose to create a hollow where the close-cut hairs lie,
and so I wanted to kiss the nape of my son's neck

and inhale the scent of him,
a trace of autumn air and rivers.

Later it was the hands of the girl with the injured wrist,
how shiny her fingernails, how the tendons moved

over her metacarpals like violin strings,
reminding me of my granddaughters' hands,

and so I wanted to twine my fingers
with theirs, to savor the tiny pulse in the thumb's web.

The last patient of the day had my grandson's gaze,
patient as a quiet sea—

and so I wanted to hold my grandson's face to mine,
to see, reflected in his green eyes, all these images

repeating themselves into infinity.

How I'm Able to Love

I'm stunned by death's absence,
by the flesh that remains, changed and yet hardly so.
I try to pretend the body's a pod or insect shell,
but attending the body after death

I see the body with all its attributions
for the first time, totally honest—
a time to satisfy that final curiosity,
the long gaze that reveals a life compressed, unalterable.

Beyond the window, rain falls. Streets below
shine like an untied black ribbon.
When my mother died, I was the one
part nurse, part daughter. I caught her last heartbeat

with my fingertips, knowing that the lungs
fail a few beats after, then breath empties them.
From long experience, I stood at the moment
just before and stroked her hair

as life moved through her as it always does—
pulling itself up through the ankles
through the bruised aorta
taking the heartbeat along, gathering the last

lungful of air and leaving nothing, all this
up through the jaw and, at the moment life breaks free,
out the open eyes. The hands respond,
as if the body wasn't robbed, but had been clinging and let go.

I don't believe in death—

even when the body mottles, even
in its closed casket, I see the body I have touched,
staring at it as I work. Only my fingers

retain the memory
of my memory. This compression is good:
it makes room for all the dead I know and don't know—
the familiar dead and the dead yet to be born.

Voices of Healing / Two

I stand on the threshold and I see
the end and the beginning in each other's arms.

—Stanley Kunitz

Day or night,
whatever the hour, it will be all shining,
our whole and broken bodies full of light.

—Margaret Gibson

Entering the Patient's Room

Knock, then enter with quiet steps,
remembering that you carry with you
news of another world.

Be attentive, noting
the placement of chairs, the presence
or absence of flowers, of cards tacked to the wall
as if to take upon themselves a measure of pain.

Look at the woman resting in bed,
seeing around her the light
emanating from her wounds; go directly
to the bedside, not afraid to take her hand
or simply sit beside.

Speak your name, or wait,
saying nothing. Remain steadfast,
while the hospital clock offers its silent hours.

Let her mind and her body be all that matters.
Let this time be sufficient to the task at hand.

Stoned

Marion asked for grass. You know, she said. It's true.
It's not the dying, but the pain.

Her friends brought in an ounce,
and when Marion grew too weak to build her little cigarettes,

I'd assign a nurse to help.
One day, the supervisor stopped outside our patient's door.

Smell that? she asked.
I shook my head.

You must be used to it, she laughed, *the smell of death.*
Then I could smell it too—

behind the pungent smoke, a scent
slightly off, a little edge to it, like old perfume.

We didn't speak.
Around us, cancer-killing poisons dripped slowly into veins;

everyone was turned and turned again, to keep skin
from breaking down where ribs and bones

poked through, and all the patients' wounds were bound.
Here's what I remember: how Marion laughed

as we nurses with our flimsy cures
pushed every chair against her door

to keep death out. And when we couldn't,
how Marion called us. Hungry. Stoned.

Marathon

A mob of runners breaks
over the Verrazano bridge, three
in front set the pace along avenues
lined by cheering crowds and plastic bins
of ice and Gatorade. Then come
the stragglers, arms and legs and hearts
pumping, their flung-off shirts
fluttering into the gutters.

The tree limbs are bare in Connecticut
where solitary runners pace themselves
along deserted roads—a man
with a bald spot, cranberry Polartec;
three women jog, their streaked
blonde hair untethered as smoke.

In the hospital, a breathless woman
runs her marathon, unaware
of shouting crowds or how shed leaves
smell half burnt. She discards,
like too-heavy clothing, the warm
jacket of memory, the light blue scarves
of joy. Once she walked on a glacier,
once on the wide path to the Villa Borghese.

Now, like the others, she sprints
toward the bright tape of the finish line.

The Nurse's Pockets

When patients are told they are dying
they say something simple:
I've had a good life or *Who will feed my cats?*
It seems harder on the doctor—
he waits outside the door, stalling,
until the patient confronts him.
So, Doc, what's the verdict?

Soon, a nurse comes to bathe the patient.
There is only the sound of water
wrung from the warm washcloth,
the smell of yellow soap
and the way she spends time praising
the valley of his clavicle, his hollow mouth.

Then, a morning when the patient leaves,
taking his body. The nurse finds nothing
but the bed with its depression,
its map of sheets she strips.
In the drawer, gumdrops. A comb
woven with light hair, and a book
with certain pages marked.

She takes all these into her pockets.
She has trunks in every room of her home,
full of such ordinary things.

Follow-Up: Women's Clinic

Alicia sits on the exam table,
        freckles scattered across her nose,
lower lip

pushed out over clear braces.
        She is twelve, with dark brown hair.
I sit at her feet on my rolling stool,

both her nurse and her confessor.
        The young man came into Alicia's house
while her mother was working.

We don't know and Alicia won't say:
        Did he cajole? Did he
cover her face?

Alicia shivers
        beneath the paper drape and stares
at the beige clinic wall.

In the emergency room
        they opened her legs in the light's glare,
scraped under her nails, swabbed

her throat, raked a tiny comb
        through her pubic hair.
They drew blood,

and sent her home.
        How can I help you, I ask.
I'd rather he killed me than raped me,

is what Alicia replies.

       I reach up, enfold her hands.

I too had to learn that my body was mine.

I help her down,

       give back her skirt, her white cotton *camisa*.

Outside the closed exam room door

Alicia's mother and I wait,

       two women standing guard

while Alicia dresses.

It Is August 24th

and at last I'm leaving the clinic
with its faded paint, its finally empty waiting room.
Good-bye to the women and their screaming children,
good-bye to the pregnant blonde whose water
broke early at twenty-five weeks
after a coke binge she finally confessed to.
I'm leaving that tone in my voice
as I probed her vagina and quoted statistics of loss,
her uterus foul with bacteria. *From what?*
I wanted to ask. *From an all night party, his oily fingers?*

Walking into the sun past "Women's Health,"
past the dried scum on the pavement
where they scuff out their smokes,
tear gum wrappers into a hundred paper swans—
on my tax money, I say later to friends, *on my tax money*—
my skin lets go of that blonde, the bloody water
that blasted apart her thighs and filled my shoes
as I opened, carefully, with one hand's fingers
the bluish lips. I think about her as I pass a man
dressed in a no-color sweatshirt, his eyes
twin blue stones.
He says *hi* so low I almost turn.

I'm used to being polite
to every patient who looks into my eyes
as if they were my friend, so I answer
hi, and walk on. There is the soft suck of gum soles
as he falls in behind me, the sound
like sticky amniotic fluid drying on the floor.
After her exam, the woman lay back

and drew up her knees. I'm better than her,
I thought, as I dropped the speculum
into the bucket, peeled off my latex gloves,
hands pale, knuckles without her jail-blue tattoos.
I know this is hard, I said,
in that way one woman has
when she turns away from another woman.

Suck, suck, our shadows walk,
light wavering around us like the fringe of flesh
that rings the vagina. What should I do?
Walk faster? Turn to stare? Run
to the alarm box, the security man, wondering
how *he* feels today,
how much better than me as I punch the buzzer
once, twice, over and over?
I see the woman in the clinic
turn toward me, eyeliner like thumbprints
under her eyes. I say, *the baby*
will probably not survive.
This is some fucking mess, she says, my car
on the far side of the ramp, the man
right behind me, both of us knowing
that I am a woman
like any woman—
just skin and hair and that sharp primal cry.

Diagnosis HIV

I don't know why I always say
what I think she wants me to say
when she asks if this infection—
these sores, these lesions, this bad prognosis—
is the result of love she made
with the man now her husband
or could it have been another man
and does this infection prove
that she's bad, something she
has suspected all along,
or maybe it was just bad luck
or could it be, she asks me, punishment
for the way she beat her children
telling them *shut up, shut up,*
and wouldn't it be better, she asks
if she herself was never born,
her own mother on the streets
like a forecast of her life?—
but then she says, *still,*
I want to live. I've learned my lesson,
and isn't my whole life about to change?
and every time she asks, I say,
yes, yes. I'm absolutely sure it will.

To Make Nothing out of Something

Driving to work, I listen to a CD,
poets reading poems about the dailiness of life:

one walks her dog in falling leaves;
another washes plates after a family reunion.

Something in their voices suggests that poems
are music, all in a minor key, chords of grief

or the sudden crescendo of memory
that makes the poets sound oddly short of breath.

I wonder if they've attended a workshop called
How to make something out of nothing,

because when I park my car, the words evaporate,
little smoke wisps trailing after me into the hospital

where doctors and nurses chant their own rhymes,
stanzas without metaphor, their subjects ponderous

but their voices so incredibly light it seems their desires
are only mortal: to make nothing out of something—

as if the spread of cancer was a mid-morning stroll
and the rebellious breast a marriage easily severed.

Then, down the hall, I walk unannounced into the room
where a man cries because his wife's nodes are positive,

and she, delirious, tries to pluck her body clean
while the intern, not yet expert,

explaining everything, rocks on his heels,
and rocks and rocks and rocks.

Mastectomy

A long pale woman
in the sea at night, her breasts
move with her breath,
   up into two moons
and down.

The doctor takes her hand,
   together, starfish,
they cup her breast.

He kisses her with knowledge:
Histologic, he hisses
into her teeth, spits *fatal*
on her tongue.
   She tastes it.
Her skin moves her bones.

He tosses survival rates
into the sky, calls men
out of nowhere.
Splashing through the water,
   they whisper
sleep words, *Fluothane*,
   and she rises.

Her breast, shucked
from the muscle of her chest,
   shrivels
in a stainless basin. Nothing,
a shell it sinks to the sea floor.

The woman wakes
    to the drone
of the doctor's voice,
his litany of statistics.

I'll tell her the human words:

    hope

        love

After Work, We Talk About Patients

Sitting at the kitchen table, coffee cups
warm in our hands and the day over,
my husband begins.
Outside, night has blotted out the trees.

He tells of a woman from Cambodia.
Weeks ago, a burning in her head,
then dizziness in crowds. Today
she complained of chest pain,

how the tranquilizers didn't help.
All her tests were negative. He stops
and takes a cookie from the jar.
She can't sleep, he says.

All she thinks about is Phnom Penn,
the man who was her husband.
My husband pauses.
I pour more coffee. My turn.

In the clinic, I say, my first patient
was a woman with visions in the night.
She'd had three children, lost
in their apartment building fire.

Another woman I examined,
age twenty-nine, had scars across
her arms and back. When I asked
she couldn't recall the details—

her only memory was pain. And

the last patient today cried when I felt
what she'd described as a red hot stone
buried in her breast. Our house falls silent,

except for the furnace, sparking off and on.
Outside, it begins to rain.

The Dark Marks

When I go to wash my lab coats,
the ones I wear to the clinic of women's health,

there they are, those dark marks on the collar,
crescent moons that appear no matter how I soap and shower.

We are all stained—doctors
in surgery, residents in their scrubs, nurses

holding the newly born.
Haven't we all said *maybe six weeks,*

when it would only take three days, or
it seems we've gotten it all, when there it was, all along?

I scrub and scrub, and yet no matter the washed hair,
the perfumed neck, the good, good intentions,

these dark marks remind me we are flesh:
mouths and hands and bodies glorious,

even as we harm. Imperfect, even as we heal.

The Circulating Nurse Enters the Operating Room

Let her not be blinded by the glare of the spotlight
or distracted by the tangle of plastic tubes,

the stink of anesthesia waiting in its multi-chambered
monolith of sleep. Let her stand beside her patients

and look into their eyes. Let her say, *we will take care of you.*
Let her understand what it is to be overcome by fear.

Let her secure her mask and turn to the counting and opening,
the writing down. Let her watch closely and, if she has to,

tap a surgeon's shoulder, *watch it*, if he seems on the edge
of contamination. Let the cutting and suturing go well.

Let the blood that saturates the gauze be red; let the organs
be glassy and pink; let the sickness be lifted out

and taken away in a stainless steel bowl. Let her patients wake,
mumbling their thanks. Let the stretchers arrive

and the linens be white. Let the patients be lifted
from the thin table, waving good-bye, good-bye

as they are taken to recovery, where other nurses wait
with oxygen, with warm blankets, with eager hands.

On Call: Splenectomy

At three a.m., the phone rang.
Car crash, the OR supervisor said,
one fool on a bender.

The guy was singing even
under anesthesia, every breath
volatile as the gas piped

into his lungs. We tipped
the table almost upside down
to keep the rancid ooze

inside his stomach and not
all over us. Skin incision,
then fat and fascia, then

a bellyful of blood
welled up and we bailed
with basins, then our hands.

The guy's spleen was ripped
in half, his gut sprang out
like a pink snake from a can.

I handed clamps and every
stitch I had and the spot light
burned down on us like fire.

It took hours to sort vessel
from nerve, to fit the knobby
liver below the ribs again.

I've taken pity on you,
left out the really awful part.
But you should see how quiet I am,

cinched in the passenger's seat;
how carefully I slice bread
into my bare hands;

how I curl on my left side to sleep.
And these stories—
how I tame them on the page.

Waking

There is nothing
and then, everything at once.

The recovery room hums like high tension wires
or a neon sign blinking
          Isn't this a miracle,
          isn't this a miracle?

You have returned from that vast sleep
during which you forgot the doctor's voice.
Count backward, it said, and you obeyed,
as if you had a choice.

You slid into death's false pocket
jingled like change
to haggle the price of a grave—or so it seemed.

Now armies of hummingbirds
buzz your veins. You hear a radio,
the clock's exaggerated tick.
You've been reborn to skin on sheets,
pain's fire doused by needle stick.

The nurse's mother-face wavers before your eyes.
All the rest, white lies.

Taking Care of Time

Yesterday it was a thousand small coins
ringing in your pocket—your hand dipped in, scooping three
at a time, giving them away. Sometimes, you'd drop one
in the lush grass, unaware it was lost.

Today time comes in a different disguise:
a bolt of fine silk, vermillion or blue, you measure it
carefully, like a woman preparing to sew.

Tomorrow, *watch out*, it comes as thunderstorm,
slant rain, February blizzard that drives you inside.
Insomniac, you pace
and curse the glow of computer screen, television, radio.

Soon enough, time may be difficult to recognize.
You might mistake it
for an elderly coughing man or a woman overrun with grief.
Do not stop your ears against its cry—

return any small change;
cherish every moment under the leaden sky.

Index of Publications

New (N)
Taking Care of Time (TCOT)
Leopold's Maneuvers (LM)
Details of Flesh (DOF)

Ensō   (N)

Voices of Healing / One:

Nursing 101 (TCOT)
Selling Kisses at the Diner   (TCOT)
Mornings We Rolled Pills into Fluted Cups   (TCOT)
Surgical Rotation   (TCOT)
The Nurse's First Autopsy   (TCOT)
Psychiatric Rotation   (N)
What the Nurse likes   (DOF)
The Condition of the World, August 1997   (LM)
Women's Clinic   (TCOT)
Alchemy   (TCOT)
Every Day, the Pregnant Teenagers   (LM)
Nunca Tu Alma   (LM)
Examining the Abused Woman   (LM)
The Good Nurse   (DOF)
The Body Flute   (DOF)

Voices of Home:

The Smoke We Make Pictures Of   (DOF)
Blood Clot   (DOF)
Four Masks   (DOF)
In High School I Was Obedient   (N)
Entering My Parents' Home   (N)
Washing Mother's Hair   (N)

The Last Heartbeat   (N)
Mother's Gloves   (LM)
I Wear Her Red Coat Home   (N)
When My Father's Breathing Changed   (LM)
Any Life   (N)
In Mother's House   (N)
Like Mother, Thirty Years before Her Death   (LM)
The Brightest Star Is Home   (LM)

Voices of Desire:

Details of Flesh   (DOF)
Hooked Up   (TCOT)
It Was a Good Year for Dreams   (TCOT)
Young Woman on a Precipice   (N)
Ritual Bath   (DOF)
March 28, 2001 / March 28, 1945   (LM)
Lot's Wife   (LM)
Partial Detachment   (LM)
Late Afternoon Nap   (N)
Almost Fifty   (N)
The Jar Beside the Bed   (LM)
Leaving the Aquarium   (N)
Shipwrecked   (LM)
To the Husband Who Stands at the Sink,
   Intent on Shaving   (DOF)

Voices of Suffering:

Suffering   (DOF)
The Nurse's Task   (DOF)
To the Mother of the Burned Children   (DOF)
Falling Temperature   (LM)
Visiting the Lightning Struck   (TCOT)

Distracted by Blackberries   (TCOT)
Hemorrhage, 3 a.m.   (DOF)
Angel of Mercy   (LM)
Patient in Surgery, 7 a.m.   (DOF)
The Barking Dog   (DOF)
A Patient Tells about Her Suffering   (TCOT)
I'm Afraid of the Brief Empty Space   (TCOT)
Becoming the Patient   (TCOT)
The Ant's Reprieve   (TCOT)

Voices of Faith:

The Vocation of Illness   (TCOT)
The Next Word You Say   (N)
Then It Was Simple   (LM)
On the Radio   (N)
At the Bedside of the Dying   (N)
Night Nurse   (DOF)
I Want To Work in a Hospital   (TCOT)
God and the Blueberries   (LM)
Rain Tree   (N)
Scattering Her Ashes   (N)
The Swan by the Mall   (LM)
Snow Geese, Like Angels   (N)
Absolution   (N)
Holy Thursday   (N)

Voices of Letting Go & Holding On:

Leopold's Maneuvers   (LM)
Parturition   (LM)
Water Story   (LM)
On Not Loving Your Children   (DOF)
She Opens a Book of Poems   (N)

Staring into the Point where the Tracks Meet   (DOF)
Ear Examined   (LM)
Reading in Hayestown Elementary School on Wednesday   (N)
First Love   (N)
Everything in Life Is Divided   (LM)
How I Imagine It   (DOF)
Dreaming for the Blind Goat   (N)
Moon Watching   (N)
It Was the Second Patient of the Day   (N)
How I'm Able To Love   (LM)

Voices of Healing / Two:

Entering the Patient's Room   (N)
Stoned   (TCOT)
Marathon   (N)
The Nurse's Pockets   (TCOT)
Follow-Up: Women's Clinic   (TCOT)
It Is August 24th   (LM)
Diagnosis HIV   (TCOT)
To Make Nothing out of Something   (LM)
After Work, We Talk about Patients   (N)
Mastectomy (N)
The Dark Marks   (TCOT)
The Circulating Nurse Enters the Operating Room   (TCOT)
On Call: Splenectomy   (TCOT)
Waking   (TCOT)
Taking Care of Time   (TCOT)

About the Author

Cortney Davis began her career in healthcare as a nurse's aide, then as an OR scrub tech. After graduating from nursing school, she worked as an RN in Intensive Care and in Oncology. Again returning to university, she became a Nurse Practitioner, working in cardiology and pulmonary practices, and for many years in women's health. In her writing, she examines how we care, or fail to care, for one another—the written word becoming the perfect place in which the act of caring becomes a way of keeping, revealing the mysteries of the world. Having been both a nurse and a patient, she believes that a patient's room is a sacred space.

Her honors include a National Endowment for the Arts Poetry Fellowship, three Connecticut Commission on Tourism and the Arts Poetry Grants, the Prairie Schooner Book Prize in Poetry for *Leopold's Maneuvers*, the Wheelbarrow Poetry Prize for *Taking Care of Time*, two Connecticut Center for the Book Awards (in Non-Fiction and Poetry), an Independent Publisher's Benjamin Franklin Gold Medal in Non-Fiction, a Tillie Olsen Creative Writing Award, and six Books of the Year awards from the *American Journal of Nursing*. In 2007, she was awarded a Nightingale Award for excellence in nursing. In addition to nursing credentials, Cortney holds a BA and MA in English. She was selected to be the first poet laureate of Bethel, CT, 2019-2022. For more information, visit www.cortneydavis.com.

This book is set in Garamond Premier Pro, which had its genesis in 1988 when type-designer Robert Slimbach visited the Plantin-Moretus Museum in Antwerp, Belgium, to study its collection of Claude Garamond's metal punches and typefaces. During the fifteen hundreds, Garamond – a Parisian punch-cutter – produced a refined array of book types that combined an unprecedented degree of balance and elegance, for centuries standing as the pinnacle of beauty and practicality in type-founding. Slimbach has created a new interpretation based on Garamond's designs and on compatible italics cut by Robert Granjon, Garamond's contemporary.

For additional information on the work of Cortney Davis,
visit www.antrimhousebooks.com/authors.html.
Copies of this book are available at all
bookstores, including Amazon.